André Braber

W9-BCN-780

WALK
ON
THE
WILD
SIDE

Also by Dennis Rodman:

BAD AS I WANNA BE (with Tim Keown)

WALK ON THE WILD SIDE

DENNIS RODMAN

with Michael Silver

Delacorte  Press

PUBLISHED BY DELACORTE PRESS
Bantam Doubleday Dell Publishing Group, Inc.
1540 Broadway
New York, New York 10036

Copyright ©1997 by Dennis Rodman

All rights reserved. No part of this book may be reproduced or transmitted in any form or by any means, electronic or mechanical, including photocopying, recording, or by any information storage and retrieval system, without the written permission of the Publisher, except where permitted by law.

The trademark Delacorte Press® is registered in the U.S. Patent and Trademark Office.

Library of Congress Cataloging in Publication Data
Rodman, Dennis, 1961–
Walk on the wild side / by Dennis Rodman with Michael Silver.
p.   cm.
ISBN: 0-385-31897-9
1. Rodman, Dennis, 1961– . 2. Basketball players—United States—Biography. 3. Life skills—Handbooks, manuals, etc. 4. American wit and humor.   I. Silver, Michael, 1965–
II. Title.
GV884.R618R63 1997
796.323'092—dc21
[B]   96-52389
                                 CIP

Manufactured in the United States of America
Published simultaneously in Canada
Book designed by Susan Maksuta-Santoro

June 1997

10 9 8 7 6 5 4 3 2 1

BVG

This book is dedicated to all the people in the world, alive, dead, and yet to be born, who have dared to be different. From Adam biting life's apple to Elvis shaking up the nation; from Lincoln raising the torch for racial justice to Jimi Hendrix blasting against the boundaries of convention. **I CARRY THE TORCH OF FREEDOM FROM THE PAST TO THE FUTURE.** Just as the flag waves free, you should free yourself and Dare to be Different.

Love,
Dennis Rodman

CONTENTS

WALK
ON
THE
WILD
SIDE

One

Make
Every
Night
New
Year's
Eve

he final seconds of the most outrageous year of my very strange life are whizzing by like shooting stars, and **I am the** LIGHTHOUSE **in the eye of the storm,** a messenger amid the mayhem.

It is New Year's Eve, 1997, and thousands of freaky people at the Chicago Navy Pier are looking up to me, hoping I'll escort them through the big moment. Judging by their delirious screams and manic motions, they seem to approve of my expensive costume. **I'M DRESSED as a sort of psychedelic Cleopatra, complete with a gold gladiator's helmet,** a purple-feather Mardi Gras mask, a jeweled necklace, a sparkling cape made of gold and purple sequins, a shield hanging over my private parts, and gold-painted, lace-up pumps. My legs are shaven, my makeup is divine, and my smile is as wide as the oversized tour bus waiting outside for me and thirty of my friends.

`So how could I not be happy?` A few years ago, I didn't know if I'd be alive for 1997, much less the guy ringing it in with a serious bang. In my roller coaster of a life, I've had some of the worst, least-eventful New Year's Eves of all time. On more than one of them I can remember sitting alone in a dingy room, WATCHING THE BALL DROP IN TIMES SQUARE, squinting at a half-broken, black-and-white TV and wondering whether the countdown signified a fresh start or a continued sentence.

WHEN YOU'VE HAD SO MANY YEARS OF EMPTINESS AND PAIN, YOU WANT TO CELEBRATE THE GOOD ONES FOR ALL THEY'RE WORTH. That's why I dropped $80,000 on this gala spectacle and brought in one of my favorite bands, Candlebox, from Seattle to headline the entertainment. It's the reason I flew out friends from all over the country, bought up two floors' worth of rooms at the Ambassador Hotel and rented a tour bus stocked with enough liquor to satisfy a blues-musicians' convention. And it explains why I searched theatrical-costume shops throughout the Chicago area for my Cleopatra gown, then had one made for a cool $10,000.

It's **IMPOSSIBLE** to put a **PRICE TAG ON INNER PEACE** and **FULFILLMENT,** and that's why the cost of this New Year's extravaganza isn't even making me flinch. As I survey the decked-out ballroom below—the round lights creeping up the massive pillars, the hundreds of balloons above, the mounted speakers ready to blast so forcefully the old wooden floors below will shake—I know this is a moment I'll never forget. The spotlight is on me as I grab the microphone. I hear only my voice, the crowd's screams, and the steady beating of my heart. There is no clock above as the countdown begins, but no matter. I will put the year to bed.

THIS IS MY TIME.

"We got 20 seconds in this time now," I hear myself saying.

"Okay . . . 19, 18, 17, 16, 15, 14 . . ." I pause to hear the audience's chant, taking it all in, not wanting it to end. "Ten, nine, eight, seven, six, five, four, three, two, one, YYYYyyeah! Happy New Year, Chicago. ¡Olé!" The balloons come down and Candlebox takes the stage, ready to rip this mother up. "I know y'all came out here to see me," I yell into the microphone, "but fuck me—how 'bout Candlebox?" I drop the mike as Peter Klett cranks up his guitar and Kevin Martin breaks into "Simple Lessons" and the madness of 1997 begins.

SIMPLE LESSONS, THE STORY OF MY LIFE. I have so many of them to share, and though the messages are basic, the learning process was a bitch. **It took me thirty-two years to find myself** and even now, at thirty-six, **I'M STILL LEARNING**

CLEOPATRA WISHES EVERYONE A HAPPY NEW YEAR

ON THE FLY. I hope no one else has to go through all the pain, discomfort, and confusion that I did in pursuit of this knowledge. I hope no one has to go through one night as bad as some of the New Year's Eves I experienced as a kid.

Growing up in the projects in the Oak Cliff section of Dallas, I knew New Year's as just an excuse for people to fire their guns and do violent, reckless shit. In other words, it was a lot like any other night. I saw so many people die during my childhood it was ridiculous, often because they were in the wrong place—the projects—at the wrong time. Back then, the wrong time was all the time. Who knew if you'd make it through the New Year, let alone the next day?

To anyone who knew me back in those days, the thought of me counting down the end of 1996 to more than 3,000 people seems absurd. I was one of the **SHYEST DUDES IN THE WORLD,** too scared to talk to almost anyone, even people I knew well. I existed in my own little fantasy world, and nobody else could come in. People talked to me in the projects, mostly to cap on me or tell me how funny-looking I was. I guess I did look pretty strange, with my big ears and pressed-in nose and skinny frame, and I just let their insults go and kept to my business. It hurt inside, but I WAS **TOO SHY AND INSECURE** TO FIGHT BACK. In projects, there are always a couple of whipping boys who get teased mercilessly, and I was one of those kids.

Back then, I COULDN'T GET LAID in a

morgue with a fistful of $100 bills. I was so ugly, shy, and clueless, there was just no way it would happen. To make myself feel better about things, I entered into a pact with three friends when I was seventeen: We would hang out together, just us guys, without dating any girls. The pact lasted several years, but it would have dissolved much earlier if one of us had been confronted with any hope of action. I didn't drink, either, so it wasn't like I was out on the town carousing. I kept to myself and kept my mouth shut, and nobody seemed all that interested. My mother, Shirley, was busy with work and my younger sisters, Debra and Kim, were already accomplished basketball players. I was just FUNNY-LOOKING DENNIS with the NO-DATING PACT.

It's scary how little I remember from those days. I think I've blocked a lot of it from my memory because **it's just too hard to go back there.** It wasn't all misery. I had my share of good times, but they were so different from the glamorous moments I'm experiencing now. When I was seventeen I managed to score an old, beat-up Monte Carlo and that car was my pride and joy. I got involved with this Monte Carlo Club, an unofficial group of people that would meet in McDonald's parking lots or places like that and cruise around. There'd be a hundred Monte Carlos zooming together around the streets of Dallas, looking for adventure. I don't know what exactly I was looking for, I just knew I was looking. Life couldn't be this limiting, it just wasn't possible. There had to be something more in store for me.

At seventeen, I saw the world from a far different vantage point than I do now. For one thing, I was much shorter. When I graduated high school I was only 5-11, nine inches shorter than I am today. The popular kids, the athletes, looked down on me literally and figuratively. **INSIDE I HAD ALL THESE BIG THOUGHTS, BUT THEY FELT TRAPPED INSIDE MY LITTLE BODY.** I wanted to spread my wings and fly with the eagles, but I was STUCK SCAVENGING THROUGH TRASH with the other junkyard dogs.

I had dreams like anyone else—dreams of being in the spotlight, of having people notice me. But those dreams seemed so far from reality that I never really took them seriously. Mostly, I lived day-to-day. My main goal was not getting crushed by reality. I caught fun where I could, tried to dodge the bullets and thought mostly about my next meal.

It looked like I'd be caught in that cycle forever—or until I ended up dead, in jail, or on drugs. But I was saved by fate, and by the Holy Spirit, who graced me with an unmistakable sign. All of a sudden, I started growing . . . and growing, and growing and growing. I had never wished I was taller or given it much thought, but now it was like I had a mandate from the heavens: *Instead of* wasting your life, *you will journey down a path of self-exploration.* And because you are tall, basketball will be your vehicle.

So, as if I had no choice, I started playing basketball, and I began blossoming as a person. THE BASKETBALL

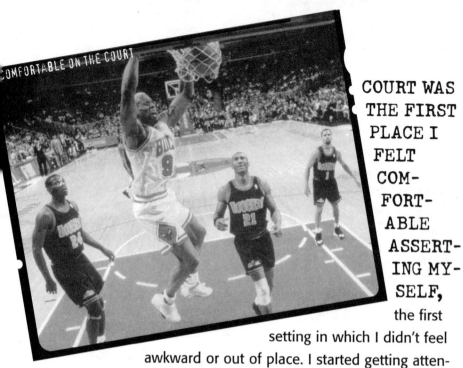

COMFORTABLE ON THE COURT

COURT WAS THE FIRST PLACE I FELT COM- FORT- ABLE ASSERT- ING MY- SELF, the first setting in which I didn't feel awkward or out of place. I started getting attention from people, and I liked it—even if I didn't know how to respond.

Basketball took me to Durant, Oklahoma, where I played for Southeastern Oklahoma State University and met my best friend, Bryne Rich, and another lifelong brother, Billy Penz. I lived with Bryne and his family in nearby Bokchito, and though we seemed like an odd couple to most people, we were really very alike—raw and scared and aware of death, and just starting to come out of our shells.

Bryne and Billy had been off dove hunting with Billy's brother, Jeff, and another friend, Brad, when Bryne's gun accidentally fired a shot into Brad's stomach. Billy and Jeff ran back to town to get help while Bryne stayed with Brad, watching him get

8

weaker and weaker. Brad ended up surviving a few days in the hospital, but he was in bad shape, and he knew he was gonna die. All of this freaked out Bryne to the point of despair. He was thirteen, and his world was a dark and haunted place. He didn't smile for months, and his parents didn't know what to do. His older siblings were all out of the house by then. Mr. and Mrs. Rich were thinking about adopting another boy so that Bryne could have a companion.

It was at this time that Bryne went to the basketball camp at Southeastern Oklahoma State. His mom was late picking him up, and he and I shot baskets together and hit it off. When his mom drove up and honked her horn, Bryne ran out and asked if he could have a friend over for dinner. She was so thrilled to see him excited about anything that she said yes immediately. Then he came back into the gym and asked me over. When I walked out, Mrs. Rich looked like she had seen a ghost. It was so quiet, you could hear a jaw drop.

But the Riches took me in as a member of their family and gave me the love and discipline I needed to survive. *I was out of the* **PROJECTS,** *but I wasn't out* **OF THE WOODS.** Here I was at twenty-one, hanging out with a couple of white teenagers, dealing with racism and small-town gossip and just trying to get by. I worked at Buddy Spencer Ford, buffing cars for a few bucks an hour. I entertained myself by stealing car batteries and clothes, or by going to the go-kart track in Sherman, Texas, and racing against Bryne and Billy, or by playing poker at the home of Don "Duck" Taylor, a middle-aged madman whose house in Bokchito was like a miniature casino.

Somehow, I made it to the NBA, and then all my problems appeared to be solved. But I was soon confronted with an even harsher brand of pain, **_THE PAIN THAT COMES FROM LIVING A LIE._** Even though I had money, fame, and two championship rings with the Detroit Pistons, I was still too scared to let loose and live the way my heart was telling me to. **I was caught up in trying to fulfill an image that wasn't me, and it damn near killed me in the process.** I went through severe depression and despair, and one night in 1993 I sat in the parking lot of The Palace, the Pistons' arena in Auburn Hills, Michigan, with a loaded gun and contemplated blowing my head off.

From that moment on, I made the decision that I would go out

SHOWING OFF THE REAL ME

on my terms, and life has been fantastic. **The CRAZY GUY you see now, with the MULTICOLORED HAIR and the TATTOOS and the NOSE RINGS and the WOMAN'S WARDROBE and the ALL-NIGHT PARTIES, is not an act BUT THE REAL ME.** After being anonymous all those years, of course I want attention, and I can't argue with the shitload of money I've made since my transformation. But what this is really about is the progress I've made on the inside, how I've found the courage to be what I really am. I feel like I've missed out on so many magical moments. Now I'm making up for lost time.

I'm like the kid who goes away to college and realizes he has no more restrictions. He can sleep where he wants, with whom he wants, or not sleep at all. Everywhere he goes is a new adventure, everyone he meets a new potential friend, and he wants to cram it all into a relatively short stretch. I am that kid, only I have millions of dollars in the bank, and a hell of a lot of people are paying attention. But the main thing is, I'm doing the things I should've been doing all along.

Once I let loose, I made a very important pact, this time with myself: **MAKE EVERY NIGHT NEW YEAR'S EVE.** In other words, every night of your life, and every day, should be a celebration of some sort. Because you just don't know how many more you'll have thrown your way.

Have you ever spent New Year's Eve alone?
If so, you know exactly why I decided to go all out for this one.

When you've had even one awful, lonely New Year's Eve, a hundred amazing parties like the one I threw to ring in '97 won't make up for it.

As it turned out, the party wasn't enough for me. Though I thrive on the commotion of public give-and-take, I sometimes reach my boiling point. **DEEP INSIDE, I'M STILL THAT SHY KID WHO'S ONLY COMFORTABLE AROUND HIS CLOSEST FRIENDS.** The circle of sickos I've accumulated over the years wouldn't work for everybody, but through their craziness my friends keep me sane. One thing we have in common is a zest for adventure. This is true of Bryne and Billy, who can drink like a pair of great white sharks, and also of my business manager, Dwight Manley, who doesn't touch alcohol but is constantly pushing the envelope. Sometimes my friends don't get along and drive me nuts by competing with each other—this is one of the downsides of my increase in fame and exposure. But on New Year's Eve everyone was in a good mood, and I knew a conventional party night—even one of MY party nights—wouldn't do.

After midnight, we left my party and went to Crobar, my favorite club in Chicago. The place was packed like Bill Gates's wallet, and we were celebrating with an endless procession of kamikazes, beers, and Jagermeister shots. *The WOMEN WERE SEXY, and the GAY MEN LOOKED HOT.* You had to yell to be heard by the person next to you, which was cool, because there was a lot of funny shit being said at very high volumes.

We cut out of there at 4 A.M. and piled back into the bus, which had twelve bunks and a private room in the back. There were about ten of us left, and I didn't want the party to stop. There was no basketball practice on New

LAYING LOW IN THE MOBILE MORGUE

Year's Day, and I felt a sudden need to escape from the mayhem and go to a sacred place that would soothe my soul. I whispered something to the driver, told everyone to get some rest and headed for the back room for a quick work-out with my friend Stacie. We were all asleep when the bus reached its destination more than an hour later, and when we woke up, people looked out the window and found themselves outside a riverboat casino in Joliet, Illinois, which is where our story picks up.

Cousin Al, one of my craziest friends, is a hard-bitten man in his fifties who makes the guys from Goodfellas look like pussies. He hooked up with Bryne and Billy in Dallas a few years ago and when he and I met, we quickly realized how dangerous we were together.

Al—or Cuz, I like to call him—has a vicious hangover. He is not alone. Bryne, having left his girlfriend Amy behind at the hotel, is practically comatose and has to be rousted from his bunk. Billy is an even bigger mess. He is not a popular man with our driver, Yogi, who took exception when Billy rose in the wee hours of the morning, staggered toward the rest room and ended up pissing all over the hallway instead.

This isn't a bus, it's a mobile morgue.

But we rally, as we always do. After a very sketchy buffet breakfast, we get on the boat and resume our party. I'm playing craps; Bryne, Billy, and Al are watching the bowl games and re-thinking their bets; the others are upstairs sucking down Bloody Marys and telling stories. People on the boat are surprised to see me, but they're mostly into their gambling and pretty much leave me alone. I go upstairs to the boat's upper level and sit with my friends, joining in the punch-drunk laughter. This is great: I'm not the center of attention, just a vital cog in an un-stoppable party machine. **I'm free to be myself, and I'M SECURE IN WHO I AM—in the moment, of the moment.** This is all I've ever wanted, really. I'm down $10,000 for the day, and I have a shit-eating grin on my face.

It's going to be one hell of a good year.

THE DENNIS RODMAN DICTIONARY

Over the years I've developed a unique vocabulary that suits my bizarre lifestyle. This list should help you understand my voice.

—Big 'N (*noun; pronounced "big-gun"*): A term of endearment, usually applied to someone in my inner circle.

—Homer (*noun*): *Same as Big 'N,* but usually uttered toward a person with redneck tendencies.

—June (*verb; usually pronounced Jooooooon"*): All-purpose verb: to rock, to go all out. Can mean "to have wild sex with." Also June (noun): Term of endearment, as in, "What's up, June?"

—Schnay: Synonym for "No," with emphasis.

—Nay: Shortened form of schnay.

—Schnuck, schnuck (*random expression, said together quickly*): Expression of approval or excitement; sound simulates the noise made by bedsprings bouncing during wild sex in Las Vegas hotel suite.

—Get Solid (*verb*): To perform in an emphatic and successful manner.

—I'll be there in 15 minutes (*saying*): I'll be there in an hour and a half.

—I'll call you right back (*saying*): I'll call you never.

—Cuz (*noun; short for cousin*): Term of endearment, especially for Cousin Al or Cousin Louie, two friends from Dallas.

—Cuz, can you cover me? (*request*): You're picking up the tab—deal with it.

—Yo (*expression*): You will listen to Pearl Jam music while waiting for me to resume our telephone conversation.

—What do you think? (*question*): Hell, yeah.

—Speak (*command*): Please say what you have to say right now.

—Click (*sound made by telephone*): Our conversation is over, and quite abruptly.

—Scaraboche (*or Scarabuche*): An endearing term for pest.

—Scamorche: Softened version of Scaraboche.

Two

Follow the Music of Your Soul

I like MY MUSIC LOUD, I like MY AL-
COHOL HARD, I like MY WOMEN HOT,
I like MY FOOD SPICY, and I like MY
SEX NASTY. DOES THAT MAKE ME A BAD
GUY?

Contrary to what some people would have you believe, I'm not some media creation whose goal in life is to cash in on your perceptions of my weirdness. I'm not a confused, abused puppy either. It took me thirty-two years to find out who I really am, and now that I've done that and I'm no longer living a life of bullshit, I want to have some fun. For so long, I was scared to do the things that drifted through the back of my mind. I wanted to take chances and explore the different sides of my personality. I was curious about sex and drinking and breaking rules and living recklessly. But I was too afraid that others wouldn't approve of me and I'd be an outcast, so I kept my fantasies under wraps and tried to blend in.

Now I'm finally being me, and it feels so natural and exhilarating. I'm not pretending to be anything that I'm not. Some of the things I do may not be for you, but to me this is the best way to live my life at this time. I really don't even think of myself as famous. I'm just an average person who likes to have a great time, all the time. I actually forget that I'm Dennis Rodman, and I like that. **HONESTLY,** *you can take away the* **MONEY,**

the CAMERAS *and the* PEOPLE KISSING MY ASS, *and* I'D STILL BE TRYING TO LIVE THE SAME BASIC LIFE.

My lifestyle is essential to my happiness. As my popularity has exploded over the past couple of years, many people have wondered if my freaky behavior is just an act. They think I'm just a marketing genius who has figured out how to shock the public and is laughing all the way to the bank.

The question everyone wants to know is this: Is Dennis Rodman just a master of manipulation, or is he really like that?

FUCK YES, I'M REALLY LIKE THAT.

IT FEELS GOOD AND IT SELLS BOOKS

That may not be what some people want to hear, because it forces them to deal with the truth. I'm not just some tripped-out Barbie doll that can be reduced to a series of clichés. `I like dressing up in women's clothes because it makes me feel good` and brings out my feminine side, not because it sells books. **I like going to gay bars and hanging out with** QUEERS, TRANSVESTITES, **and** TRANSSEXUALS because I find them a hell of a lot more interesting than the boring-ass dudes I see in locker rooms and on basketball courts. I like dyeing my hair and posing naked and showing off my tattoos because it's a way of expressing my freedom and individuality. I live my life with abandon and I live it openly, because I'm not afraid to let people see who I am.

Don't get me wrong—the money is nice, and I don't mind the attention. I'm definitely somewhat of an exhibitionist, and it gets me off when I know my behavior is forcing people to open their minds. I like the fact that I'm making people deal with issues, like homosexuality in sport and in society, that they'd rather flush down the toilet. **I'M IN A BETTER POSITION TO DEAL WITH THE WRATH OF SOCIETY THAN MOST PEOPLE, AND I'M HAPPY TO HANDLE THE PAIN.** If I'm the one getting stared at and ragged on and joked about, that's all well and good, because I can take it. Nobody— not a referee, *NOT A MEDIA* `DICKHEAD` *LIKE BOB COSTAS,* not some drunk asshole in a bar—can make me feel as shitty as I've felt in the past. I've seen it all, bro. When you've been poor, homeless, sexually abused, and victimized by racism, it's hard to feel threatened by public ridicule and disapproval.

There are a lot of gay athletes in the world who are too scared to come out of the closet. There are a lot of athletes that totally want to be wild and crazy, but they just feel that they can't, because society and the sports world won't let them. If I can help to change all that, to pave the way for people in all walks of life to be more true to themselves and accepting of others, then that's a pretty cool thing.

But the real reason I walk on the wild side is for myself. I have a lot of different sides to my personality, and I'm very thoughtful and intelligent. Still, this is what it all comes down to: Life, to me, is like one of those funky-looking crawfish you find down in New Orleans. The best thing to do is boil it in the spiciest broth imaginable. Then you take that sucker, rip its head off and suck the juice right out of it.

If you think it's all about money, you're missing the point. I've been poor as soot in my life and still managed to have fun. I'VE BLOWN THROUGH CASH LIKE IT WAS KLEENEX AND HAD A HELL OF A GOOD TIME DOING IT. I was pretty much broke before I hired Dwight and got traded to the Bulls in 1995. Then things picked up again. I'm trying to stockpile cash now so I can take care of my daughter, Alexis. But I have my limits. In a lot of ways, I'd be happier making about $2,000 a week than the millions I'm making now.

I never thought any of this shit would make me money. I

thought it would be totally the opposite—I thought it would cost me whatever money I had, one way or another. I can't even imagine doing what I'm doing to make money. Most people don't expect athletes to do crazy, whacked-out things. That's probably why other athletes don't do them—at least publicly—because they're scared it would cost them money. I'm not driven by cash. It's like saying John Holmes was driven by acting. The man had a 14-inch penis; he was doing what he needed to do in those porno films, just like I am when the camera is watching.

Another myth is that I'm obsessed with what everyone else thinks of me. There's a part of me that cares, but all I really notice is whether people are thinking about me at all, not what they think. I think it's cool when people talk bad about me. There's an old saying, "The only bad publicity is an obituary." I like that. I don't trip out on other people's negativity. When you see things from my perspective, you can't.

I don't sit around calculating my next move, trying to figure out the best way to shock the public or make headlines. How boring does that sound? No, I'm too busy livin'—**L-I-V-I-N**—as they said in the movie *Dazed and Confused*. I just close my eyes, breathe slowly and deeply and let the music that beats inside me tell me where to go.

It's one of my basic rules: Follow the Music of Your Soul.

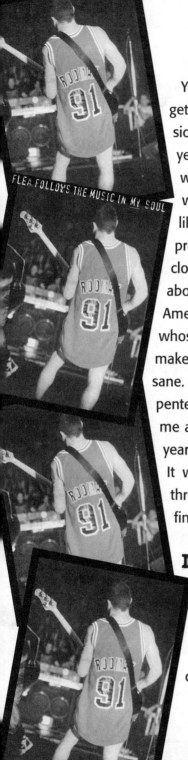

FLEA FOLLOWS THE MUSIC IN MY SOUL

Dennis Rodman

You have to go through a lot of bullshit to get to the point where you can hear this music loud and clear—believe me, I know. A few years ago, I only recognized it on occasion. I was caught up in the music I thought people wanted me to follow. They wanted me to be like lite rock—no edge, nothing offensive, predictable groove. I couldn't wear freaky clothes or have too much fun in public or talk about controversial topics. I had to be the All-American athlete, a milk-drinking role model whose only goal in life was to win. This is what makes people comfortable, but it drove me insane. Growing up, I listened to shit like the Carpenters and Captain and Tennille, and it took me a long time to shake that vibe. Until a few years ago, I was like the Air Supply of the NBA. It was hard work, but I managed to break through that crap and crank the stereo and find my true groove.

The music of my soul is **LOUD, PULSATING,** and **UNAPOLOGETIC.** That's why I love Pearl Jam so much, and rockers like Alice In Chains, Red Hot Chili Peppers, Live, Metallica, and Soundgarden. I like a lot of different types of music, but it all has one thing in common: **AN EDGE, A PASSION, AN ATTI-TUDE.** I like the Smashing Pumpkins for that reason. I think Rage Against the Machine is fan-fucking-tastic, because they force people to think about who holds power in society and what choices they make. I like some rap and R&B and even some things that are kind of mellow, just for a change of pace. Sometimes I need a change, because I listen to music so much, it's scary. When I'm driving in my truck, when I'm working out at the Bulls' facility, **WHEN I'M HAVING SEX,** when I'm straightening up my house ... whenever, there's a good chance I'll be listening to tunes. Some-times I think I actually like gearing up for sex while listening to loud Pearl Jam better than I like sex itself.

Certain musical figures go beyond the scope of sound and take their magic to an-other dimension. There are three in particular that I admire: Frank Sina-tra, Elvis Presley, and Jimi Hendrix. **SINATRA IS THE BOSS**—just listen to any-thing he sings, and you can tell he's the one in the center of

WORMING MY WAY BACKSTAGE WITH
THE RED HOT CHILI PEPPERS

the action, the one who's making things happen, rather than re-acting to them. My favorite song by him is "My Way"—I feel like he could've written that for me. I'd love to take NBA commissioner David Stern as my prisoner, strip off all his clothes, rub lipstick and makeup all over him, dress up like Frank and sing to him . . . "I did it my way." It would probably be my last act as an NBA player, but it would be worth it.

Some of my friends think I'm the second coming of Elvis, and I must admit there are some similarities between me and the King. Like Elvis, I'm a southern boy who lifted himself out of a poor upbringing and hit the big-time. **When I was growing up in the projects and things seemed bleak, I ALWAYS LOOKED AT ELVIS AS PROOF THAT ANYONE WITH THE RIGHT COMBINATION OF FLAIR, TALENT, DRIVE, AND LUCK CAN BECOME IMPORTANT IN AMERICA.** Once Elvis made it, he turned his back on the mainstream entertainment crowd and instead surrounded himself with the "Memphis Mafia," a close-knit group of folks from back home. The Memphis Mafia allowed Elvis to be somewhat approachable in public, and I, too, have a bizarre set of friends and associates that I like to place around me in order to feel comfortable. The King had a habit of going to the same places and getting the same things. I do this, too—I just don't order quite as much food as he did. Elvis was into "taking care of business," and that's the way I approach my life, especially the basketball court—it's great to fuck around, but there are times when business has to be tended to, because it's the reason all the other shit exists.

The King and I both have been able to transcend race in America, which is no easy thing to do. HE DIDN'T **GIVE A SHIT WHAT COLOR YOU WERE,** AND NEITHER DO I. He hung out with lots of black people, and I have mostly white friends. I've experienced my share of racism— from people calling me "nigger," to getting pulled over by the police for driving a nice car, to having rocks and cans thrown at my car when I lived in Oklahoma—but *I've never viewed life in black-and-white terms.* Maybe it's because I felt like a reject in the black community before I became a basketball star, but I've never really felt comfortable being characterized in terms of color. I saw Elvis bring all different types of people together because he was a damn good singer, and that's the way it should be for anyone.

Elvis managed to make it as an actor, basically by acting like himself, and that's what I'm trying to do now that I'm entering the final stages of my basketball career. There's also the Vegas thing. Elvis obviously ruled that town, and it has become my home away from home. I love the wild energy, the scent of sin, the total devotion to fun. I'd love to star in a remake of *Viva, Las Vegas.* It's the one place I can go hang out, do my thing, and not feel any weirder or more out there than anyone else. **Once Elvis became a fixture in Vegas, he started dressing up in rhinestone-studded sport coats and funky shit like that. Obviously, I**

can relate to having a strange, trend-defying wardrobe.

Lately I've been fascinated by Hendrix, a dude I truly dig. Not only was he the monster-blaster of all time on guitar, he lived his life the way he wanted to. I love how he would do things like show up on the Dick Cavett Show WEARING A PURPLE ROBE AND NO SHOES, probably tripping out of his mind, and JUST FLAUNT HIS FREAKINESS. I can relate to the way he scared people with his wild words and actions. Think of that song, "If 6 Was 9," when Hendrix says, "White-collar conservative flashing down the street, pointing that plastic finger at me . . . I'm gonna wave my freak flag." Considering the political and social climate of the time, imagine how that made white-collar conservatives feel when they heard that blasting on their children's stereos.

Jimi was especially scary to those individuals who don't know how to deal with black folks. Yet Hendrix had mostly white friends and fans and existed in a largely white world—again, I can understand what he was going through, because my situation is very similar. Just as Jimi wasn't supported by black radio, or by black people in general, I was just a funny-looking nobody who couldn't get a date until I made it to the NBA. Even now, three quarters of the black community isn't supporting me. They don't think I'm black—**EVERYONE THINKS I'M MORE WHITE THAN BLACK**—and they believe that I don't represent the black community and all that crap. **WHY LAY THAT TRIP ON ME?** I'm the one who's well-adjusted. I see everybody as equal. I don't care what color you are. I hope blacks will come to appreciate me in the long run, just like they finally accepted Hendrix as a brother years after his death. Because I'll tell you one thing, **they love that MOTHER-FUCKER RIGHT NOW.**

Sometimes, I think I was born a little too late. If I had a time machine, I'd go straight to Woodstock and blend in with that incredible vibe. The sixties was a great time for freaks and people living balls-out, and I think I would have fit right in. If I had been old enough to check out Woodstock, I'd be taking off my clothes and dancing in the mud and fucking in the grass and getting off like everyone else. **YOU HAVE TO EXPERIENCE THE HISTORY OF LOVE.** I would love to have put Day-Glo paint all over my body and worn big floppy hats and come-fuck-me clothes. When I wear stuff like that, it makes me feel more wanted and more independent and in tune with my inner spirit. Back in the sixties, everyone got all wrapped up and tangled up in that web and I would have been right in there.

It's no coincidence that the sixties coincided with the heyday of the electric guitar. Rock music was the language of an entire cultural movement, and along with rap, it's still the form of expression that's closest to the pulse of the people. If I wasn't a basketball player, I'd probably be in a rock band. I COULD SEE MYSELF AS A DRUMMER **FOR SOME**

CRAZY-ASS GROUP, THRASHING ABOUT ON THE SKINS AND LAYING DOWN THE BEAT FOR EVERYONE ELSE TO FOLLOW As big a rush as it is to score a basket or grab a rebound or draw a charge in front of 17,000 screaming people, I think it would get me even more jacked up to rock 'n roll onstage.

Being onstage during a live rock performance is a mind-blowing experience. It makes you feel like a supreme being. I know, because late in the summer of 1996 I took the stage during a Pearl Jam performance in Augusta, Maine. It wasn't planned, but it turned out to be one of the most amazing things I've ever done.

I got to know the guys from the band a few years ago, mostly Jeff Ament, the bassist. It was a total thrill for me, because I feel like *their music captures my inner spirit. IT'S POWERFUL, PULSATING, PASSIONATE, and PAINFUL,* yet there's a streak of positivity running right up its spine. I mean, you've got a heavy-metal lead guitarist (Mike McCready), a punk-rock rhythm guitarist (Stone Gossard), a wild bassist (Jeff), a no-bullshit drummer (Jack Irons) and Eddie, who has the most amazing voice of all time. **THEIR SONGS TELL A STORY, AND I CAN ALWAYS RELATE TO IT.** Eddie doesn't shy away from pain, and he manages to capture a wide range of emotions. As I said, I listen to all different types of music, but I mostly rock out to Pearl Jam. Their MUSIC to me is LIKE HEROIN TO A JUNKIE. The guys in the band help feed my spirit by sending me special

Walk On The Wild Side

CDs—live recordings, outtakes, demo sessions, and stuff like that.

It was really easy to get to know Jeff, because he's just a regular cool dude. If you didn't know who he was, you'd never think he was some big rock star, because he doesn't act like he's hot shit or he needs attention or anything like that. He's a pretty big basketball fan, like most of the guys in the band. Their name used to be Mookie Blaylock—he's a player for the Atlanta Hawks, and I guess they liked his name. Their first album, "Ten," was named because that's Mookie's number.

Eddie was tough to get to know, because he's a really private person who only puts himself out there when he's onstage. Hard as it is to believe, I'm actually very shy, too, so Eddie and I both sort of played it low-key around each other. But in the summer of '95 we started hanging out, and we really hit it off. Eddie's a lot different than I am. He tries to fight his celebrity. He wants things to be the way they were before he hit it big. I think it's a futile struggle, but I respect the hell out

EDDIE VEDDER HELPS US CELEBRATE THE CHAMPIONSHIP

of him for the way he tries to live his life. It's tough bringing him around hectic scenes; we usually do better hanging out when it's just the two of us.

But when you get Eddie onstage, he's a natural-born show-man, as I found out during that show in Maine. I had just flown back from Arles, France, where I'd been acting in *Double Team*, a film with Jean-Claude Van Damme and Mickey Rourke. It was my first major acting role, and man, was I wasted—even though I had barely partied over the previous several weeks. I got to New York with my friend, Stacie, and my buddy, Dwight, and we took a private plane up to Maine the next night. We were hang-ing out backstage during the show and the band was totally rocking. **I THOUGHT MY EARDRUMS WERE ABOUT TO EXPLODE, AND AT THAT POINT I WOULDN'T HAVE MINDED AT ALL.** I had a glass of red wine in my hand and I was feeling pretty good about life as I stood there watching Eddie get off. It was late in the show and they were playing, "Alive," and Jeff and Stone were running around the stage, as usual, and Eddie was wailing his lungs off. He got to that part I love—"Is something wrong? she said. Of course there is..." and I just wished I could be part of it, somehow. This might have been one case where I really did crave the atten-tion—or maybe I just want to be a rock star at heart, like a hell of a lot of other people.

So, when he sang, "WHO ANSWERS? WHO ANSWERS?" it all of a sudden hit me. *I was overcome with this rush of energy, and it was like I was possessed by an alien being or a ghost or something. I knew then that I was the one who answers, so I walked out onstage and brought Eddie the red wine.* There was no way I could have anticipated the reaction. **PEOPLE WERE *GOING NUTS.*** I got one of the biggest ovations I've ever received. **PEOPLE WERE DELIRIOUS**—it was like they wanted to rip my clothes off and just take me, right there. It was one of the most awesome moments of my life. I practically had an orgasm onstage.

The coolest thing about it was the way Eddie reacted. He jumped up onto my back and rode around on me, piggyback style, while he was singing and screaming into the microphone. I should have screamed along with him—it was my big chance—but I was overwhelmed by the moment. So he's riding up there on my back, and now the microphone cord is getting all tangled up around me, and Eddie's just getting crazier and crazier, and then that little madman does a back flip off of me and onto the stage. It was a great move, except the microphone started choking me and I couldn't breathe—so now I was having one of those asphyxiation orgasms, which was cool, but it was still pretty scary. Finally, I managed to untangle the microphone from my neck, and I cruised offstage and back into civilian life.

It's a moment I know I'll never forget, and one I'm able to relive often, because Eddie gave me a tape of the show right after

ONE OF THE MOST AWESOME MOMENTS IN MY LIFE

it ended. I didn't have anything to play it on, so he gave me his Walkman, with his initials marked right on it.

It was a once-in-a-lifetime experience, but I'm not willing to settle for once. **I'VE GOT TO FIND A WAY TO GET BACK TO THAT MOMENT, IF IT'S THE LAST THING I DO.**

Go
With
What
Got You
There

*b*ooze, limos, private clubs, rock stars, freaks, sushi, strippers, and some of the finest-looking women in America. It was all there waiting for me on a balmy night in Seattle, and I wimped out like some sort of paranoid politician.

I PICKED ONE HELL OF A TIME TO HAVE AN IDENTITY CRISIS.

It was June 11, 1996, and it seemed like the whole world was watching everything I was doing. In the previous few weeks I had posed naked in *Playboy*, released a best-selling book, cried on Oprah, allowed a *Dateline NBC* crew to follow me into clubs and modeled a G-string for Cindy Crawford on MTV's *House of Style*. And oh, yes, I had played a little basketball, too, winning my fifth consecutive NBA rebounding title and helping the Chicago Bulls to the league's all-time best regular-season record, 72-10.

OPRAH MADE ME CRY . . . I MADE HER SMILE

Now it was the playoffs, and we had been even more dominant. Out of fifteen games, we had lost only one. People were calling us the greatest team of all time, and with good reason. I know we were one of the greatest spectacles ever, thanks partly to my multicolored hair, nose rings, tattoos, wild wardrobe, and outrageous behavior. I admit it: I'm not the safest guy in the world. I live my life like the 24-second clock is ALWAYS about to expire. I've done a lot of crazy things, especially over the last few years. But on the night of June 11, under the glare of a white-hot spotlight, I did something completely, UNDENIABLY IN-SANE.

I turned my back on the behavior that makes me what I am.

We were one game away from winning the NBA title, and I was playing my ass off. The Seattle Supersonics couldn't stop me, bro. We were up three games to none, and while everyone knows Michael Jordan is the greatest basketball player ever to roam the earth, people who understood the game realized that I was the one killing the Sonics. They had no answers for my rebounding and defense, and some of their players, especially Shawn Kemp and Frank Brickowski, were so mind-fucked by my wild energy, I had them hypnotized. After two victories in Chicago, we blew them off the floor in game 3 at Key Arena in Seattle. One more victory and I would own my third world championship ring, and I knew exactly where this one would go: On my middle finger, so I could flip-off my former employers in

San Antonio who broke the promises that organization made to me about renegotiating my contract, then trashed me publicly when I violated even minor team rules.

I wanted this last victory so bad, and I buckled under the pressure. With everything swirling around me like a billion vampire bats, I temporarily went brain-dead.

I know it's hard to believe, but I was confused about my identity. Yeah, I'm the guy who likes to dress up in women's clothes and go to gay bars and get in touch with my feminine persona. Yes, I'm a hard-living, free-thinking freak who can't be chained down, classified, or reduced to some cliché. I thought I knew all that in Seattle, the city where Jimi Hendrix learned to blow people's minds and Kurt Cobain blew his head off. But when I got that ring within my grasp, I was the one who lost his mind.

DAVID ROBINSON AND THE SPURS CAN KISS MY ASS

For some dumb-ass reason, I stopped partying. After one of the most reckless, out-of-control social seasons in NBA history, I tried to stay in and be a good boy. The first two nights in Seattle, I had gone out with some of the coolest people I know—Eddie Vedder, Jeff Ament, and Stone Gossard from Pearl Jam; Bryne Rich, Cindy Crawford, who was sitting on my lap at one point...just to name a few.

Eddie and Jeff had been with me in Chicago, too—actually, they were with me for a lot of the playoffs. They would tear up the town with me all night, then have the balls to root for their hometown Sonics, sometimes while sitting in my seats during the games. I respect them for their loyalty and lack of hypocrisy. Besides, if it wasn't for Pearl Jam, my life would be a hell of a lot less fulfilling.

I love to party as it is, and for someone like me, the NBA Finals are like a traveling Mardi Gras. Plus, my popularity had exploded in the past year, and I was reveling in the madness. Everywhere I went people screamed and clawed at me, like I was one of the Beatles landing in America in 1964. Women, and men, were sticking their hands down my pants in public and whispering wild sexual offers into my ears. It seemed like everyone wanted to meet me, and I do mean everyone.

One night in our hotel bar in Seattle, some blond woman who seemed to have a buzz on came over and said she wanted to meet me. She seemed totally excited, almost like she was checking me out. "I really admire your work," she told me. She said that she loved the way I carry myself and assert my individuality. I turned away and asked one of my friends who she was. "She's an actress," my friend said. **A PORNO STAR?** "No," he said, "it's Meryl Streep."

Meryl went on complimenting me for an hour. She was a really nice lady. "I liked you in *Death Becomes Her*," I told her. I didn't even know what other movies she'd been in. There was really nothing else I could say, so I just sat there and listened to her tell me how fabulous I am and how much she loves the way I act.

Every night was full of surprises, until I pulled the biggest one of all. June 11 was a Tuesday, the day before game 4. My friends all wanted to go out and rage. Of course they did. That's why they're my friends. But I wimped out. I TRIED TO PLAY MR. FUCKING CONSERVATIVE. Speeding down the fast lane on the road to glory, I pulled off at a rest stop. Instead of following my heart, I listened to a devilish voice inside my head.

I stayed in and tried to be a good boy, but that just ruined my whole groove. I'm a person who operates on vibes, and when the vibes are good, I exist in the zone of love. That's why I dress the way I do—because it makes me feel free, and it makes me feel desirable. When I feel that way, I can thrive in whatever I'm doing. There aren't that many things I hold sacred—my daughter, Alexis; my inner spirit; my work ethic—but I definitely believe in the sanctity of my groove. I'm not some CD that can be programmed with a bunch of separate, digitized commands. I'M A VINYL ALBUM, BRO. I need to have that groove.

I'm constantly bombarded with advice from people who think they know what's best for me: coaches, teammates, referees, NBA big-wigs, businessmen, agents, broadcasters, columnists, family members, and friends. Some of them mean well, some of them don't. But the people who know me best understand one thing clearly: If there's one thing I hate, it's someone telling me what to do. Often, I'll do the opposite, just to show that I'm not a puppet. This time, like a fool, I listened to some of those voices that I usually ignore. After all I've been through, it's amazing I was foolish enough to go against what I knew in my heart was right. But I've never claimed to be perfect, and I guess you could say this was just another mistake in a thirty-six-year life of risks.

I don't know what the hell I was thinking. I just said to myself, "I've got to focus on winning this next game," and I played it mellow. I must have come home from dinner before midnight. Then I got about seven hours of sleep—the longest continuous stretch of sleep I'd had all season. And the next day I went out there and sucked. Even worse, we got our butts kicked. That freaked me out even more, and stupidly, I laid low that night, and the next night, too. On Friday night we went out and lost game 5, sending the series back to Chicago. People were starting to question whether Seattle could do the impossible and become the first team ever to come back from a 3-0 deficit. The flight home to Chicago was not a pleasant one. There were some tight assholes on that plane. Instead of acting loose and confident, people kept to themselves and barely said a word.

As we jetted over Idaho in the wee hours of Saturday morning, I realized what an idiot I'd been. If I wasn't such an antidrug guy, you'd have thought I was stoned or something.

I'm not saying we definitely would have clinched the series in Seattle if I hadn't restricted myself so dramatically. I'm just saying the whole team, for whatever reason, seemed to tense up as we reached the brink of victory. Like most teams, we play better when we're not stressed out, and nothing stresses me out more than trying to be something I'm not. If you believe in karma—and I definitely do—it's easy to understand what happened. It took me a few days, but I finally figured it out.

For one thing, **I HAD BROKEN ONE OF MY CARDINAL RULES: *GO WITH WHAT GOT YOU THERE.*** As applied to the NBA Finals, that means don't all of a sudden piss your pants because the stakes are higher. If you're the type of guy who goes home to his wife and watches a movie on most nights during the season, do the exact same thing in the playoffs. If you're into hanging out at strip clubs and watching pornos featuring 400-pound women in black pumps, keep doing just that. And if you're me, and you're nearing the end of an eight-month binge that would send most people to the Betty Ford Clinic... well, you do what I did beginning that next night in Chicago. I rounded up some of the craziest bastards I know and went to my favorite sushi restaurant in Chicago, and started doing Sake Bombers the way a dying man in the desert drinks water. We ended up at Crobar, where they have a bondage rack and men will stand there writhing in pain while voluptuous women pour burning wax onto their nipples, and people in elevated cages dry-hump each other to the

beat of **ear-splitting techno-house music played by A LESBIAN DEEJAY NAMED PSYCHOBITCH.** We went to breakfast at Third Coast, a great place in the Gold Coast district, and when I walked out the door it was light out. **I knew I was ready for game 6.**

Sure enough, we went out and got solid and **WON THE DAMN TITLE.** It was come high, all comers welcome. After all those years I lived my life based on other people's expectations of who I should be, I had suffered a temporary relapse and survived.

The real reason I was so damn pissed off at myself for wimping out during that stretch of the finals was because of all people, I should have known better. I was the guy who didn't get laid till he was around twenty-one because he was too shy and insecure about himself—and because women thought he was too ugly. I was the guy who spent seven seasons in the NBA playing the image game, trying to be the good samaritan, the good boy, the saint, God's child. Finally, in 1993, I sat alone in a pickup truck with a loaded gun and decided I was through with all that bullshit. Instead of killing myself, I made a promise: From now on, ***you are not going to skip down that Yellow Brick Road of ass-kissing and finger-crossing.*** You will have heart, brains, and courage, and you will have one hell of a good time. As Lou Reed would say, "Hey, babe, take a walk on the wild side." And do it with one hell of a smile on your face. That's what's gotten me through these past few years. That's what's going to get me through the rest of my life.

Four

Never
Sell
Out

*O*f all the stupid shit that takes place in the sports world—and believe me, there's a lot of shit—the most ridiculous thing of all is the way athletes obsess about their image. By this point, most people are hip to the fact that **the majority of athletes are PRIMA DONNAS, EGOMANIACS, and WILD MEN,** spoiled babies who get special privileges and do whatever the hell they can get away with and sleep with everything in sight. So exactly what image are they trying to protect?

It's sad that athletes are afraid to let loose in public because they think the average person out there really believes they're these wholesome individuals who are role models. Role models, my ass. Most athletes try to get models in bed, and that's about it. If you want to view me as a role model for anything, **TAKE THIS PRINCIPLE TO HEART:** NEVER SELL OUT. PROTECT YOUR INTEGRITY WITH YOUR LIFE.

Fans aren't as stupid as they're portrayed to be—they watch the news and read the newspapers, and they know how many of their sports heroes are assholes. Either that or these image-conscious superstars are born-again Christians who can't shut the hell up about how holy they are. The perfect example of this is David Robinson, my former teammate in San Antonio. Mister Robinson used to be a wild man, but now he's Mr. Rogers.

No matter which way you slice it, **ATHLETES ARE AS BORING AS C-SPAN.** I have fun going out with some of the guys on the Bulls—Luc Longley, Steve Kerr, Jud Buechler, Bill Wennington—but I pretty much try to avoid hanging out with athletes at all costs. Most of them are so scared to express themselves and so focused on sports as the heart of their identity that they just sit around and talk about themselves. Then there are the types who are quiet and goody-goody in public, but as soon as the camera's off, they're wild and crazy. Those people are hypocrites, and I don't find them interesting at all.

What the hell is the big obsession with image, anyway? So you can get endorsements, and make money? Whoopdie-doo. How much is the price of a man's soul? I'd rather live my life the way I want to and not try to hide who I am. If people want to pay me under those terms, then we can talk.

LOOK, there isn't too much in this world that is meaningful and lasting. They can take away your money, your job, your freedom,

SELLING SHOES
BUT NOT
SELLING OUT

47

and your peace of mind, *but they can't take* **YOUR INTEGRITY IF YOU WON'T LET THEM.** Never Sell Out, and Never Kiss Ass—whether you're famous or just trying to get through the next set of bills. I know what it's like to be poor, and the quick fix is very tempting. But it's just not worth it.

You'd think people in my business wouldn't be so willing to prostitute themselves for a quick buck, but that's not the case at all. So many athletes are whores who will put their name on anything for a paycheck. Offer the typical star player a chance to plug a new brand of cyanide-flavored cereal for kids, and if the price is right, he's all over it. Every day some lame, bullshit company calls up and wants me to do this or that, but you've got to sift those things out and limit yourself to a few endorsements you can live with. **You can either be like Dennis Rodman or Michael Jordan,** who has a ton of endorsements. We have different views on the matter and I can understand that it's good to get paid, but, whether you take his approach or mine, I still think you should **BE TRUE TO YOURSELF.** I also think that the image he uses to sell all that stuff traps him. He's the classic example of a guy who I imagine would love to let loose like I do but always has to watch himself because he's protecting his image. Yeah, he takes home millions and millions of dollars from endorsements, but is it really worth it? How much is enough?

Every one of the companies I do stuff for I can at least say puts out a good product that I'm willing to buy myself. I was

TWO VIEWS ON ENDORSEMENTS

wearing Oakleys way before I was affiliated with the company. I got introduced to Jim Jannard, the head of the company, and he thought I was cool, and I told him I really dug his shades. That's what led to me endorsing Oakleys.

You know what product I'd love to put my name on? The Brush. You probably haven't heard of The Brush, but a lot of athletes—and the women who screw them—know all about it. The Brush is this Chinese herbal potion that you smear onto the backside of your dick and it keeps you hard for a long time, often more than an hour. I'd like to go on TV and pitch The Brush, and I know a hell of a lot of women who could be in the commercials with me and sell it with big smiles on their faces. I'd even demonstrate it in action if the FCC wasn't so uptight. They'd barely have to pay me anything, either—whoever the hell is responsible for The Brush, that is. It would be an honor to be associated with the product, and it would be more like a public-service announcement. It could go something like this:

Me: They say a good man is hard to find, but a hard man is good to find. I'm Dennis Rodman of the Chicago Bulls, and when I'm cooling out after a tough game, I need something to make sure my endurance remains strong. That's when I call on The Brush, for the man who never wants to leave his woman hanging.

Hot Blonde: And believe me, The Brush does the trick. Make sure ALL your men carry it, so they'll never have to spend any time on the physically unable to perform list.

I'm telling you, it would be the commercial of the year, and women would be extremely grateful. Instead of just selling The Brush in sex shops, they'd have to start carrying it at Wal-Mart and Safeway.

Some people wonder why companies would want someone as controversial as I am to pitch their products. I'll tell you why: **BECAUSE I'M REAL,** *and everyone knows it.* Consumers aren't total idiots. They can see right through someone like Shaquille O'Neal, who not only whores himself out to a million sponsors but acts like a damn fool. You'll see Shaq being interviewed on live TV and he'll say something like he just wants to be young, have fun, and drink Pepsi. Uh, yeah. No one could possibly believe that's what he really feels; it's such an obvious load of crap. He might as well dress up like a Pepsi can when he plays. **No one should want to sell a product that bad. IT'S PATHETIC.**

When I pitch, I have to do it my way. As long as a product serves a legitimate function and doesn't take its shit too seriously, I'm willing to help sell it. At the end of 1996 I shot a commercial for Kodak, and they had me dressing up in all these funky outfits. I was a candystriper in one frame, a nurse in another. The cool thing was they let me keep the costumes, and I showed up for my weekly television show that I do in Chicago, filmed live at Planet Hollywood, dressed as Nurse Feelgood. As I told the audience, "Do you know Dr. Feelgood? I made HER feel good."

The whole idea of lending your name to some corporate cause is bizarre. It's temping to take some of these offers because the money is just so easy. This was especially true early in my career, before my salary was so high. It's easy now for me to be selective; back then it was damn hard not to jump at any opportunity. Luckily, I didn't have many offers until I started getting freaky, so the temptations pretty much weren't there. I am proud that I never sold out and never kissed any ass. But it's always a fine line when it comes to people selling your name.

Even recently, I've agreed to some deals that I almost immediately have regretted, because they made me feel so sleazy. During the summer and fall of 1996, I spent four of the most useless days of my life at autograph-signing shows. I did it because I made something like $45,000 each time and I hadn't done anything like it in several years, so I had forgotten how truly brutal it is to sit there for four or five hours and put your autograph on all kinds of stuff that most of the people are going to turn around and sell, anyway.

It's hard to turn down all that money, but what you're really doing when you appear at an autograph show is selling your soul. I won't do another one for a hell of a long time, because I just feel so dirty and impure afterwards. I have all this pent-up anger and I just want to get naked and scream as loud as I can for about twenty minutes. You sit there on this stage and one by one people come up and give you something to sign. They tell you what color pen to use and where to put the signature and then they want to make conversation. I have no problem with interacting with fans, but it's just so twisted and fake when you're up there on that stage, like an animal at the zoo, and there's an endless procession of visitors.

At this recent card show I did at a hotel ballroom in Chicago, it was completely insane. There were all these parents bossing their children around, totally yelling at them, because they didn't get into the right spot for a picture or didn't move fast enough. I make my living dealing with pressure-packed situations, and I hate it when I see people freaking out like that. One mom had her kid take off her shoe for me to sign and then said to the girl, "You have to walk barefoot to the car; we can't wear that shoe anymore." Then there were these older ladies who were totally trying to flirt with me, which was pretty funny. One of them brought a copy of my first book, *Bad As I Wanna Be*, but told me she didn't want me to sign the back cover "because the buns are beautiful, and I don't want to spoil them." Her friend looked over and said, "Foul me, baby," and gave me a big, wet kiss. None of these things by themselves are that horrible, but string them together for several hours and you feel like a disgruntled postal worker, just ready to snap.

The whole autograph concept is weird. Not only do I not understand why they exist—are they proof that you've met someone famous?—I'm totally suspicious of people's motives when they ask for an autograph. If you want my signature on something and you're gonna put it in your house or collection or something like that, I can deal with it. But if you're just gonna turn around and sell it, then that's a pain in my ass. You can't even trust the kids anymore, because **parents are WHORING their kids like prostitutes.** They tell them, "Go up and get his signature, because he'll never say no to you." And then you give it to the kid, and his dad sells it. It's fucked up.

I can't stand it when I pimp myself for money. Other than being able to put something away for my daughter, it's worthless. I think it would be better to blow off most of the outside shit and just play hoops or act or whatever. I don't mind having money, but it's not the be-all, end-all for me. Sometimes, it's a giant pain in the ass.

If someone took away all my money right now, I'd deal with it. It wouldn't be the first time I was broke. I'd have to find a job, and I think I'd be able to get a job making good money somewhere and then I'd probably be happy as shit. I wouldn't have to worry about people coming into my life and bullshitting me all the fucking time and offering this and that—the unrealistics of the world. Because in a way, **MONEY EQUALS BULL-SHIT. THE MORE MONEY YOU HAVE, THE MORE AGGRAVATION AND THE MORE TRAUMA YOU HAVE TO PUT UP WITH.**

I can live on $1,500 a month. I can live pretty comfortably on that kind of money, and in a lot of ways it would be simpler. I'd just get a one-bedroom apartment, for starters, and that would be sufficient. Then I could have even fewer commitments, the crumbsnatchers would go away and I could hang out with the people who love me for who I am and not because I buy them meals or help sell their product.

When you're in a situation where so many people are throwing money at you, it's sort of threatening, because the worst thing in the world would be to get caught up in the madness and forget who you are and why people respect you in the first place. If I ever become one of those pathetic assholes who is totally obsessed with money and is willing to sacrifice his dignity, just get a gun and shoot me.

Walk On The Wild Side

There aren't that many people in this world that I admire, but the people I do all have one thing in common: integrity. They learn about themselves, they develop values and opinions and stick to them, without any fear of what others might think or of who might get offended.

In my career I've been blessed with two coaches who fit this description: Chuck Daly, who I played for in Detroit, and Phil Jackson, my current coach in Chicago. Everyone says I have such a problem with authority and am a troublemaker, but that's not the case when I have respect for the person with the authority. You can't win with people who are power hungry and want to control you just to show they can. And when you resist them, they try to manipulate you by poisoning your image. But Chuck Daly is a straight shooter, and I totally love the man. He's like a father figure to me. And *Phil is just a cool dude.* He's one sports figure who's interesting enough that I wouldn't mind hanging out with him for a while. If he wasn't married I would want to see what kind of guy he is—if he's a party animal, if he's a sex-crazed jungle man. He probably was in his youth, when he was playing basketball.

Just before the start of the 1996–97 season, I showed my appreciation to Phil by presenting him with a custom Harley-Davidson. Even though he had just won his fourth championship for the Bulls, our cheap-ass management dicked him around and treated him like a piss-boy. They wouldn't offer him what he was worth and he had to settle for a one-year contract for $2.5 million—good money, but way less than what someone like John Calipari, who had never coached in the NBA before, got from the New Jersey Nets. Phil could have told them to fuck off, and he would have gotten hired somewhere for major bucks. But he stayed in Chicago and that meant Michael Jordan stayed and I stayed, and another championship is within our grasp.

That meant a lot to me and to the team, so to show Phil that we, the players, definitely appreciate him, I got this Fat Boy Harley with a Bulls logo on it and had everyone sign it. It cost $18,000, which doesn't even begin to approach how much I value the way Phil has treated me. I think he was pretty touched when I gave it to him. Some of our sponsors were having this tip-off luncheon right before the start of the season at a hotel ballroom, and I cruised in on the bike, drove it up to the stage and presented Phil with the keys. He was totally surprised, and it was a great moment. ***PHIL'S THE PERFECT EXAMPLE OF A GUY WHO DIDN'T SELL OUT,*** and I hope he feels my appreciation every time he's out there on his Fat Boy with the wind whistling through his hair.

Another person I admire is Howard Stern, not just because he's funny as shit, but because he's not afraid to say things straight-out, even if some people say he's racist and insensitive or whatever. He just doesn't give a damn about what people think about him, and he has pulled off the greatest radio show on earth.

Howard Stern knows how to talk to people, and that's why his interviews are so revealing. He'll say to me, "You know, you

PHIL JACKSON EARNS MY RESPECT

think you're fooling everybody, but you're not fooling me. I know what you're doing all this stuff for. You want money and you want to be the king. But you can't be, 'cause I'm the king. You wish you were like me, 'cause I'm the master." I say, "Yeah, Howard. You're Jewish; you can't play basketball." And he says, "That's not true. I'm only half Jewish."

I've only hung out with him once off the air, and it was by accident. One night in the summer of '96 I walked into Scores, the greatest strip club in New York, and he was there, just having a great time. He was surrounded by all these beautiful women, and he was excited to see me, but he was still pretty low key. He's so wild when he's on the air, and it's hard to stay in a zone like that all day long. You've got to have your room to rest and rejuvenate. So we just had a mellow conversation—as mellow as you can be with voluptuous hardbodies dancing in front of your face—and he basically told me to keep living life the way I'm living it now.

Pearl Jam also stick up for their principles, even if it costs them. They don't do videos because they think it ruins the way people perceive their music. And they lost a shitload of money and got shafted on one of their tours because they went to war against Ticketmaster. God bless them for that. Ticketmaster is the king of the leeches, always adding ridiculous service charges that jack up ticket prices, and the guys thought it was wrong, so they made a stand. I respect everything about those guys. They're prochoice, they value their individuality and their freedom, and they're willing to fight for it.

There's one other person I admire, though she's not too big a fan of mine these days. **Madonna may be** RIPPING ME A NEW BUNGHOLE **in the press for revealing details about our sexual encounters, but I still look up to her,** because she's a strong person whose heart is in the right place. I appreciate the things she has done, like showing people that there's nothing wrong with being gay, and I know she's going to stick to her guns and not back down to anyone.

She's mad at me right now, but I'm sure at some point we'll see each other again and we'll talk and get past all of this bullshit. I think we can be friendly, but who knows. Maybe she'll give me the brush-off.

Or, better yet, **MAYBE I'LL GIVE HER THE BRUSH.**

Five

Give Your Life Structure, But Don't Get Strangled By It

i have this fantasy that I can live my life like a tiger in the jungle—eating whatever I want, fucking whenever I want, shitting wherever I want, and roaming around butt-naked, wild and free. In my heart I'm just an aimless wanderer who lives for the moment, but in the last couple of years I've actually found that a little structure can be helpful. It's not something I brag about, because I hate being tied down by routine, and **SPONTANEITY IS MANDATORY.** Still, I don't think there's anything wrong with a little stability, at least in moderation.

In a lot of ways, my life was easier before I had a business manager and scheduled appearances and bodyguards. I didn't even have a cellular phone or anything, and I was pretty tough to track down. One time in Detroit a few years ago I changed my phone number and purposely didn't listen when the phone-company representative told me what the new number was because I didn't want anyone to be able to call me.

You know that song, "Let the Good Times Roll"? I love that line: "I don't care if it's twelve or three, time doesn't mean that much to me." **THERE'S STILL A SIDE OF ME THAT WANTS TO GET ON A MOTORCYCLE AND CRUISE ACROSS THE COUNTRY, EASY RIDER STYLE.** I'll probably do that one of these days, but in the meantime life has gotten complicated, and I've done some things to try to cope with the insanity.

For one thing, I work out twice a day, every day—once after I wake up, and again in the evening before I go out to dinner. **This not only helps my body to stay in shape but allows my mind to regroup and maintain its groove.** It's a time when I can be alone in my thoughts and it makes me feel like I have my shit together, no matter what crazy things I might have done the night before.

I usually go to the same set of restaurants and order the same meals over and over. There are about five or six restaurants in Chicago that I go to and they all pretty much know what I'm going to eat once I get there. It may sound sort of dull, but I find it comforting. There are certain friends I call every day, and some of them call me. I even have a cellular phone, though mostly I keep it in my truck.

This stuff may not seem like a big deal. To me, it sounds very confining, but let's not get carried away. I still don't have a pager, and I refuse to wear a watch.

ARAN . . . HALF OF MY HOME SECURITY SYSTEM

I screen all my calls at home, and when I check the messages, I never write them down. I either remember the message, call the person back immediately or blow it off. I figure if it's important enough, they'll call again. It's a very liberating way of dealing with the situation.

I don't hassle with a home security system; I just have a pair of German shepherds, Aran and Katy. Anyone who dares to break into my house when they're around, go right ahead.

One of the things that scares me the most in this world is that I'll get lulled into interacting with conservative people and being around them will suck the life out of me. When I go out in public and walk into a bar or club or restaurant, I can instantly tell whether people in there feel free or whether they're restricted. I can't be around a very conservative woman or man, because it makes me feel totally structured and confined. If a person is judgmental and uptight, if he or she isn't open to new experiences or nonconventional points of view, how will that person be able to understand my crazy life? When someone tries to categorize me, I feel like a caged animal.

I can't deal with other people's boundaries, because I've had a hard enough time breaking down my own. I've got my life structured. I've got my building already. It took me a while to get that building in place. It's like the old ruins in Rome, like the Colosseum. It'll never crumble, but you have to do what you can to preserve it. I don't want anybody coming in and saying, "Okay, let's tear this down and redo it." IF YOU'RE A PERSON WHO'S **OBSESSED WITH STRUCTURE,** I HOPE YOU STAY THE HELL AWAY FROM ME, **BECAUSE *I CONSIDER YOU DANGEROUS.***

The whole institution of marriage freaks me out for this reason. I was married once, to the mother of my daughter, Alexis. If I could take anything back in my life, that would be it.

I knew getting married probably wasn't the right thing to do, but we gave it a shot for Alexis' sake. Actually, Alexis was the one who talked me into it. She was three years old at the time, and the three of us were in Lake Tahoe, just on the Nevada side of the border with California, at the Chapel of the Bells, one of those cheesy places where you can get an instant license. I waited outside the chapel for like two hours, just sitting there, concentrating. My little girl kept saying, "ARE YOU GONNA GET MARRIED? YOU GONNA GET MARRIED?" She just kept saying it over and over, and finally I buckled. It was the worst. I wish I had been drunk, cause if I was I swear I would've never even gone to the chapel in the first place.

It wasn't exactly the most romantic wedding in the world. I went into the chapel wearing combat boots, shorts, a T-shirt, sunglasses, and a hat. Then after the ceremony I went to McDonald's, got a couple of cheeseburgers, and prepared for the one-night honeymoon. The next day, I got on a plane for Europe—alone—and spent the next couple of weeks tripping around. We never did have sex on our wedding night or anything, and the week after I came back from Europe, we stopped living together.

That relationship obviously was fucked up—both of us made some mistakes, and when it comes down to it we aren't exactly soulmates. I liked her in the beginning, and after the baby came there was something there, but we weren't in love or anything. We just weren't compatible, and we got married for the wrong reasons. Who knows what I was thinking? Back then I was just dazed. I do know that after the baby came it was more like an obligation—you have to get married for the baby's sake— and that messed me up. ***I should have been honest with myself*** about my feelings for my ex-wife, instead of putting it all on the child. Now I hear my ex-wife is writing a book about our so-called relationship, which saddens me since it's only going to hurt Alexis.

Marriage in general is a tough thing for me to deal with. I'm pretty sure I'll never tie the knot again, even though I staged that funky ceremony in midtown Manhattan in the summer of '96— the one in which I dressed up in a bridal gown and married my fans. When I announced on *The Late Show With David Letterman* the night before that I was getting married, none of the people who really know me believed me, because they're aware of how I feel about marriage. The ceremony I staged in Rockefeller Center was actually very meaningful to me, but only in a symbolic sense. Unless something changes drastically, the only way I'll walk down the aisle for real is if I'm dragged.

I'll probably just have a girlfriend the rest of my life. In this day and age it's much better. I think marriage cramps both people's style. The whole idea of monogamy seems unnatural to me. **Men are like dogs, and WE WANT TO FUCK EVERYTHING IN SIGHT.** Any man who tells you otherwise is full of shit. There are some men who can fight against that and stay faithful, but what's the point? And women struggle with it, too. I can't tell you how many married women come up to me and say, "I hate my husband. I need someone who's gonna satisfy me." Married people fuck around on each other all the time.

If I could be in a marriage where both partners were allowed to sleep with other people, that would be something I'd consider. Hell, let's be honest—a lot of people would go for that arrangement. But how many people could actually pull that off? It would be difficult as hell. The only other way I could see a marriage working, for me, is if I got married to someone that lives in a foreign country, and I stayed in America. Then maybe we wouldn't drive each other crazy all the time.

What I'm really looking for is a woman who's INTELLIGENT, who's really got HER SHIT TOGETHER, and who has HER OWN GROOVE. She can't be hanging all over me all the time; she has to have her own thing going. I like a girl that's just funny as hell. She should be strong-minded, a go-getter, but not a pain in the ass who's always trying to tell me what to do or play head games. She shouldn't worry about what the hell I'm doing. She should give me my space. She should be creative and she should have some secrets, just to keep things mysterious. And, most of all, I like a girl that's spontaneous. She should be the type of woman who shows up and tells me, "Hey, let's go, right now, and cruise across the country to California on a motorcy-cle—I'll drive."

If I could find a woman like that, **I MIGHT BE ABLE TO CONSIDER BEING MONOGAMOUS.** But that doesn't mean we should be married. I don't know why people are so obsessed with marriage. It's nothing but a piece of paper. Unless, of course, you're really rich, in which case it's a power is-sue, an invitation to take half of your money. If I was gonna marry someone with less money than me, I'd ask her to sign a prenuptial agreement, and that's a major turnoff to most women.

As much as I'm down on marriage, *I think the family is a legitimate institution, and I hope to have one someday.* I'm not against a family at all. I think fami-lies keep the world stable and balanced. And you can have a family without being married. You can have a family within your own religion or within your own surroundings—the possibilities are so much greater. Just because you have a child with some-one doesn't mean you should be married. I think those days are gone. There's too much shit out there happening, too much temptation.

I personally don't want to be tied down with anybody, but I'm not hard on people who desire the family lifestyle. If I could find a woman just like me, very free-form, and we had a child to-gether, our child would be the same way. We could have a child that just doesn't give a shit about boundaries. I may well find a woman that I want to reproduce with and decide to have another child. I could totally see myself doing the family thing.

Does that mean I'll have a station wagon and a house with a white picket fence? Schnay. There's no way in hell that will ever happen. But it doesn't have to be such a dramatic adjustment. When people have kids, their lives totally change—of course they do. But that doesn't mean you can't go out and have a good time, enjoy the finer things in life, and experience life the way you have all along. You might have to alter your behavior at times, but your attitude doesn't have to be any different. You can have a structured life and a crazy life at the same time—it blends together and balances out, like a seesaw. It all fits in with my basic theory: `Give Your Life Structure, But Don't Get Strangled By It.`

If I look back at the way I was raised, I can see that I've always craved that security you get from a family unit. My mom, Shirley, loved me, but she also doted on my younger sisters, Debra and Kim, who were basketball stars and were much better adjusted than I was. I was hyper and stressed out and funny-looking and everyone used to make fun of me. It was hard growing up like that, but things ended up working out okay. I still keep in touch with my mom and sisters. I appreciate the fact that they don't ask me for shit, that they don't try to take advantage of me. Debra just moved out to Orange County to work with the Rodman

Group, the firm that manages my career, and though I don't talk to her or Kim or my mom every week or anything like that, we manage to touch base on all the important stuff every so often.

Being a parent to Alexis is hard, because my relationship with her mother is strained and I don't get to see or talk to my daughter as much as I'd like to. If I had my way, I'd have custody of Alexis. But in the meantime, I try to stay karmically connected to her, and I hope she knows that everything that one of us experiences, the other is experiencing inside.

The last fucking thing I'd ever want to do is follow the example of my father, **PHILANDER RODMAN,** who bailed out on me when I was three. **Has anyone ever had a more perfect name? It would be like if Pete Rose was named "Gamble."**

One of the worst side effects of my fame is that this guy Philander is getting all this attention and airtime, and he sits there in the Philippines, where he lives, bragging about how he's the father of twenty-seven children. Twenty-seven children! Like that's supposed to be admirable? Father's Day must be the most confusing day of the year for him. It must totally freak him out, because I don't think he deals with many, if any, of his kids. Except, of course, he wants to meet me now. I have so little interest in that, it's scary. It's not that I'm overly bitter towards the guy. He just doesn't mean anything to me, and I'm not really curious about what he's like, so why waste my time? A tabloid show actually had the nerve to bring him to a game this year, my first after the eleven game suspension. They were probably hoping to ambush me for big ratings but I sidestepped the whole show.

If I had twenty-seven children, I'd be ashamed. We all have a right to be free, but we also have choices to make, and we have to take responsibility for those choices. All I know is that I personally will take responsibility for any child I bring into this world. I can't imagine living a life of 9-to-5 hell, like many guys have to do, but I'd do whatever I had to do to put food in my daughter's mouth.

There's so much bad shit in the world, and we all have to figure out our separate coping strategies to get us through this crazy life. If that means adding some structure to your existence, so be it.

BUT WHEN THE STRUCTURE BECOMES YOUR EXISTENCE, THAT'S WHEN IT'S TIME TO TAKE A STICK OF DYNAMITE AND BLOW IT ALL TO PIECES.

Get in
Touch
With Your
Inner Freak

eaven knows I'm not the best-looking guy in the world. I've got bad skin and a wide-ass nose with two rings sticking out, and my hair is usually dyed some bizarre color. Yet millions of women want to fuck me, more women than you'd ever believe. How can that be?

I can think of a few reasons. I have money and I'm famous. And people are attracted to me because I'm different, because I play by my own rules, and because I'm a lot of fun. But the biggest reason of all, I think, is that when women check me out, they see a man who is wild and free and unafraid to explore his fantasies. They see a person who doesn't believe that anything is dirty, filthy, or impure. In other words, they see someone who will let it all hang out, whose motto is, `Get In Touch With Your Inner Freak.`

I'm sure I don't have the wildest sex life on earth, but it's not because I haven't tried. *I'VE SCREWED A LOT OF WOMEN IN A LOT OF WAYS IN A LOT OF IN-TERESTING PLACES, AND I'M NOT EVEN CLOSE TO BEING BORED OR SATISFIED.* But I'm not totally consumed by sex, because I want it to be special, not just something that's as routine as taking a shower or eating a meal. I still laugh at how Wilt Chamberlain claimed to have had sex with 20,000 women. I may be a freak, but I'm not a total whore. I mostly have sex with women I care about, and I don't even come close to doing it every day. A lot of people think I do the nasty at least 300 days a year, but it's more like 200, maybe 225. If that were true I'd be a goddam soup sandwich, just a pile of mush. I couldn't work out, I couldn't play, I couldn't do anything—I'd just be totally overwhelmed by fucking. I always visualize myself trying to have sex for 30 days straight, just with one girl, but that doesn't seem possible, either. A lot of people say, "Well, I have sex every day." Bullshit, you do. There's no way in hell. For one thing, your wife or girlfriend couldn't deal with it, because they'd be wanting something new.

I happen to love sex, and **I love experimenting and fantasizing and finding new ways to get myself and other people off.** Does this make me strange or deviant? No. Our country is so puritanical about sex it's a joke. Sex is a natural act—it's how we make babies, so what could be more natural? Anyone who tries to tell you otherwise, even your parents, your doctor, or

DRESSED TO THRILL

your priest, is completely full of shit. If you have any doubt about whether I'm right, close your eyes, shut out the rest of the world and think about it. Does the thought of doing everything with another person—especially a person you're not supposed to be with—turn you on? Of course it does, and that's beautiful. If your sex drive makes you feel guilty, that's only because it's such a hot, nasty, awesome type of urge that it seems unfair that you get to experience it, or even imagine it.

There's nothing better than having wild, uninhibited, outrageous sex with another person who's going off just like you. You're making primal noises and saying crazy things, juices are flowing and shooting everywhere, and your head is spinning so fast you're dizzy. You feel like every ounce of energy you have, all the nutrition and fluids and everything else, is just snatched out of your body. Who wouldn't want this feeling at least once in a while? I think there should be one day a month where everyone is required to get it on, either with a partner or partners or solo, whatever turns them on.

Like I told you before, men are like dogs. They'll jump on anything. They're always ready to go.

WOMEN ARE MORE LIKE **CATS.** THEY'VE GOT **INTEGRITY.** THEY TRY TO KEEP THEIR **HORNINESS A LITTLE MORE PRIVATE.** But deep inside, they still love to get it on. And when they're in heat, you better get ready, because they're gonna make you work and work and work to keep them satisfied.

I'm not telling you anything you don't already know. Everyone

Walk On The Wild Side

talks about the difference between making love and fucking, like making love is a sacred act but fucking is nasty and crude. Again, close your eyes and think about which one sounds better. Or see how you react when your partner tells you during sex that he or she wants to get fucked.

> You really can't make love as much as you can fuck. Fucking is so much better, because you let all the aggression out.

Chances are, you're gonna fuck every time. The only time you're gonna make love is if you're married, maybe on your wedding night. Or maybe after an argument, or when you think your marriage is on the rocks, or if you're feeling especially romantic. But any other time, you're fucking. There's an old saying that when you're married, you're gonna fuck the girl that you love. I mean, you can't make love to your wife or girlfriend every goddam night. That's just impossible. A lot of guys sit there before and during sex saying, "Honey, I love you, blah, blah, blah. I wish you'd be here forever." Then when they get through with it, the first thought to pop into their head is, "God damn, I'm tired, I don't want to be around your ass."

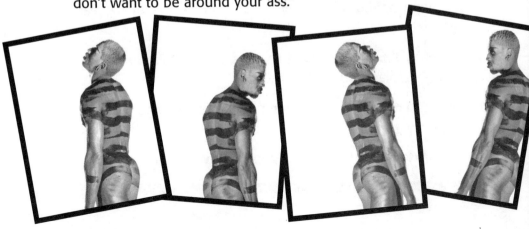

Top 10 Worst Pickup Lines

Women and men are always hitting on me and seem to think they can say anything to try to get me in bed. I've used some awful pickup lines myself, but I rarely have to break them out anymore because everyone's always coming after me. The list:

10. **Can I just touch you?**

9. **I think you're the sexiest man alive.**

8. **I'm from Detroit** (or Dallas, or San Antonio, or Chicago. 90 percent of all people who talk to me are from one of those places).

7. **I haven't spoken to you all day, but I'll fuck you now.**

6. **If I was 10 years younger, I'd be fucking you.** (An 80-year-old lady said this to me. I was like, "Whoa, okay.")

5. **I hate my husband. I need someone that's gonna satisfy me.**

4. **Remember that night we got together and I was naked and you were naked and we just wore each other out?** (Yeah, right.)

3. **Normally I'm not attracted to guys, but I'd love to be with you.** (A lesbian said that to me.)

2. **I want to do you like Madonna. If you fucked her, you must be pretty good.**

1. **Your dick would look really good in my mouth.**

One reason I'm so interested in getting laid is that I haven't been doing it for that long. I didn't have sex until I was twenty years old, maybe even twenty-one, I can't remember. It took so long because I wasn't a very attractive bastard back then—let's face it, I was ugly—and I wasn't the most outgoing, exciting person in the world. I was pretty much clueless. No one had ever really told me about the birds and the bees, and I hadn't even masturbated all that much—something I've also made up for in recent years.

I lost my virginity to this wide-body who lived upstairs from me in the projects in Dallas. I think her name was Thelma or something, and she was pushing 200 pounds. She had had a boyfriend but she wasn't too experienced, either. We were hanging out one day and it just sort of happened. She was over-weight, but she was cool. She was the girl who lived upstairs in the projects. I know a lot of people can relate to that.

So I got on top of Thelma and started going at it. Even the first time, I was able to make it last. You know I'm gonna go in there and run with the thoroughbreds. I'll be right there in the middle of the pack, because my nervous system's not that bad. When guys come too soon, it's because of anxiety. The anxiety takes control of them, and they have to let it out. I don't have anxiety, thank God. Some guys have a bad nervous system and they just blow in two minutes. To me, it's like savoring a glass of red wine—you just sip it, and you smell it, and sip it and sip a little more. *You have to make it last, and you have to feel like* **YOU'RE IN CONTROL.** *It's not* *your body that's in control,* **IT'S YOUR MIND.**

Anyway, my first time wasn't that big a deal. It really wasn't special or anything. You just go fuck. Just get in there and tear it up, simple as that. When it ended, I went back to my boring-ass life. It wasn't until I made the NBA that things got exciting.

When I joined the Detroit Pistons, I couldn't believe the sexual opportunities that came my way. All of a sudden all these freaky women wanted to fuck me, and I became more and more open to new possibilities. It was like I could do it anywhere, anytime, and believe me, I did. There were wild scenes in hotel rooms. It would be me and a teammate and two women, all on the same bed, going at it and switching off. And what tripped me out as much as anything was the way some women got off on doing it in public.

ONE TIME *I HAD SEX WITH THIS WOMAN ON A FROZEN LAKE* IN DETROIT. We were on Lake Elizabeth, right over by my house, and we just got this Nordic rush of horniness and went at it. I'd be on the bottom, literally freezing my ass off, then I'd turn her over and hump her like a dog while her hands and knees slid across the ice. The best thing about it was the way it iced my balls—that made me last forever, almost like I had used The Brush.

Sometimes I feel like the world is my bedroom. Another time, my date and I were waiting for a table in a crowded restaurant in downtown Detroit, at the top of the Renaissance building. The place was full of people. We were around the corner from where everybody waits to get their table, in this little side area, but it wasn't closed off by a door or anything, and you could hear everything we were doing. My date just said, "I want to fuck you right now," and she lifted up her dress and started jumping on me. She wasn't wearing underwear, and I was wearing jeans, so I just unzipped the old portable peephole. She got on and rode me, and there was this security guard type of guy nearby, so I called him over and gave him a hundred bucks and asked him to sort of stand guard. We were definitely making some noise, and I know some people could see us. This one couple came over and asked, "What's going on here? Is everyone OK?" The security guard said, "Everything's fine." She was up there for like twenty-five minutes, and whenever anyone would walk by she'd just kind of hold me real tight, like she was just sitting on my lap, and keep right on going.

You've heard of the Mile High Club? I'm proud to say I'm a card-carrying member. I was flying first class to Hawaii on a 747, and it was unbelievable. The first-class cabin was upstairs and it was packed

CAPTAIN OF THE MILE HIGH CLUB

with people. This woman I was hanging out with at the time was in the seat next to me, and **SHE JUST STARTED PLAYING WITH HERSELF,** just getting into it. **I LOVE WATCHING WOMEN MASTURBATE,** and it gave me a giant hard-on. She said, "Well, we can't do it here because everybody will see, blah, blah, blah," and I said, **"I DON'T GIVE A FUCK. I WANT TO DO IT, RIGHT NOW."** She's about 5-foot-4, and she just got up and jumped in my lap and started doing me in front of about twenty people. It was daytime, and there was a movie showing, but I GUARANTEE WE WERE THE MAIN ATTRACTION. I tried to play it off. She was clenching my ass the whole time and biting my ear off and I was just trying to brace myself for the explosion. That's what I call the friendly skies.

I've had sex in a lot of places—you name it. I did it on a boat dock. **I FUCKED in my car while a cop watched.** I was going for it on the side of the road and a cop came by and flashed his lights. He came over and must have recognized me because he said over the loudspeaker, "Mr. Rodman, can you please get out of the vehicle?" I was a little busy at the time, so I just kept right on going, and eventually the cop took off. The only thing better is fucking in a moving car, though it's usually better if you're not driving. In the summer of '96 I bought a Bentley with Dwight, and we immediately drove the hour from his place in Orange County to the Viper Room in Hollywood. I met some woman there and she and I broke in the plush leather interior in the backseat while Dwight drove home.

One of the all timers, though, was when I did it with this woman in her front yard as the sun came up. We had been out all night and driving around, and I said to her, "You know, when I fuck you I want you to just scream. I want you to say every nasty thing so your neighbors wake up and hear you just getting nailed." So we drove back to her house and went out there on the front yard and did the wild thing for a couple of hours, until about eight in the morning. She was screaming my name and talking dirty and putting on a show for the neighborhood. I wish her neighbors would have joined us. It could've been the ultimate block party.

I love the idea that I can just get down wherever I am and do the nasty. One of these days I'm going to jump out of a plane with somebody and we'll pull our parachute cords and start fucking each other up there in the sky as we float down to earth. That will make the Mile High Club look like the Friars Club.

IT'S GOOD TO HAVE FANTASIES, especially when others are willing to help you out by acting them out in front of you. I've seen my share of activities. A lot of times two girls will want to perform for me. They'll offer to give me a free show, and I'll say, "Knock yourself out." Two women for a guy is the ultimate dream, and if they're going to eat each other and do a full-on lesbian love act, I'm all for it. I've been to orgies and sex parties that are pretty amazing, filled mostly with rent-a-girls. It would be nice to participate, but I think my fame trips people out, so I've pretty much jacked off more than anything. If I did start to jump in, you know there'd be someone in the back making a phone call as soon as I did. But hell, it doesn't hurt me to watch.

Sometimes my partner and I will beat off in front of each other. But most of the time when I masturbate, I do it alone. **I CALL** *my right hand Monique* **AND** *my left hand Judy,* and they get plenty of action; I'd say I jack off at least twice a week. I have some porno flicks at home—hell, most single guys do—but I don't need a video or a magazine to get me off. It's all in my mind, and I usually make it last, just like sex.

COME ON IN MY KITCHEN

In addition to flatware, plates, and drinking glasses, I keep a healthy supply of sexual aids and toys in my kitchen.

THE CONTENTS OF MY CABINET:

- **The Eager Beaver Pocket Pal**
  (A multispeed vibrating, artificial pussy.)

- **Sabrina's Love Beads**
  (Beads on a string.)

- **Astroglide Personal Lubricant**

- **Mr. Prolong**
  (Ointment that extends your erection.)

- **Lover's Leash and Lover's Collar Set**

- **French Ticklers**
  (Pointed plastic stimulants to be placed on edge of penis.)

- **One-Stroke Personal Lubricant**

- **Passion Fruit Body Butter**

- **Original China Brush Liquid Incense—aka The Brush**
  (Legendary potion which, after being rubbed on the backside of penis, allows you to stay hard for a seemingly endless stretch. Deceptive instructions say, "Open Bottle, Let Stand Till Room Smell Good.")

You know what I'd love to try sometime? Beating off during an NBA game. If I was sitting there on the bench and I was thinking of something very sexual, why not? I could just slip Monique or Judy down into my shorts and make it happen. They'd probably kick my ass out of the NBA, but fuck 'em. It would be one hell of a way to go out.

Now that I'm trying to become an actor, I've thought about the concept of doing sex scenes. I think I'd be pretty good at acting those out. I don't think I'd ever want to be in a porno, because they'd probably ask me to take pills or inject myself with whatever shit they give you so that you can keep going after you come.

Most men have fantasized about having sex with a porn star, but for some reason I'm not that up for it—maybe because that's all they do, so how exciting could it be for them? Besides, I've had my chance. One night during the 95–96 season I went out with some friends to a place called Martini Ranch in Chicago, and Seka was there. If you watched any pornos during the seventies, chances are you've seen every part of Seka up close and personal. She's the one who used to do John Holmes, all 14 inches of him, and then say something like, "His come is godlike." She was looking pretty good back then, but not when I saw her. She was out celebrating her fortieth birthday, or maybe her fiftieth, and she came over and introduced herself to me. She said she wanted me to be on some TV show she had, and she wanted a picture taken with me, and she wanted to buy me a drink. She definitely wanted to fuck me. I could tell by the way she was talking. I was not at all interested, but I will say this: Her tits were a sight to behold. They were humongous, and I was definitely checking them out.

I'm getting better and better at sex all the time, but I'm far from being a master. My favorite thing about it is the way I approach everything before I fuck. To me, sex is an intense, powerful act, and my view is, Don't Dick Around When You're About to Whip Out Your Dick. **I'M VERY BIG ON GETTING IN THE MOOD.** I could be listening to Pearl Jam or Alice in Chains, which is very seductive music. When you hear Alice in Chains, it's like they're fucking you as they're playing. Their music just gives me a hard-on. Sometimes I think I get more enjoyment from listening to the music than from fucking itself. Talking dirty is also a part of it. *Every man likes to be king of the hill while he's fucking.* And every girl's gonna tell you you're great during sex. You can have the smallest dick in the world and she'll still say you're great, and there's nothing wrong with that. But I'll tell you this: If I was a girl and a guy wanted to fuck me and his dick was kind of like my pinky finger, I'd say, "Wait a minute, this ain't gonna do it. I need something that's gonna get me in a different ozone." Fortunately, I happen to be very sufficient in that department. Some of my friends call me "The Crippler," because I can really make a woman scream with pleasure.

Madonna got all angry at me over my last book, *Bad As I Wanna Be*. She said in *Vogue*, "I'm sure somebody wrote the book for him, and I can only imagine they urged him to be as imaginative and juicy as possible and to make things up." But I stand by my story and I think she's mad because I shared our relationship with the world. She can rip me all she wants but its the God-honest truth that she wanted me to eat her out the first night we were together but I refused. I don't mind pleasing a woman, but I think women in general want to please the man more than they want to get pleased themselves. Or maybe I just think that because I don't particularly enjoy going down on a woman. It's not a big turn-on for me.

If had a tongue-licker that ran on batteries, I would just put it down there and let it go. I have a lot of sex toys—dildos, vibrators, potions, and stuff like that—but the tongue-licker would be the ultimate machine. I'd turn it on and put it down there for about 20 or 30 minutes. There's no way I'd ever go down there with my tongue for that long, but the tongue-licker could get the job done.

In general, I'm pretty open to different kinds of sex. **I LIKE IT WHEN people get kinky, AND I LIKE IT WHEN THINGS GET ROUGH. MY BASIC RULE IS THAT ANYTHING GOES IN BED,** though there are times when even I get grossed out. This one woman I've

been with a lot is a total freak who knows no boundaries. She wants it all the time, and she likes it every which way. Sometimes she wants to be pissed on or shit on. I know April flowers bring golden showers, or something like that, but it's not really my scene. And asking someone to shit on you is just ridiculous.

I like a woman who just doesn't care. That really turns me on. ***I WANT SOMEONE WHO IS SEXY AND VERY SURE OF HERSELF, VERY CONFIDENT AND JUST TOTALLY IN CONTROL OF EVERYTHING.*** She should also be able to let it go. She can be voluptuous, she can be anything you want her to be at any time, boom, at the snap of a finger. She can fly like a bird and say, "I don't want you to fuck me, just kick my ass."

It's hard for people to talk about rough sex, but my feeling is that as long as both parties are up for it, there's nothing to be ashamed of. I think it's cool when a girl is slapping the shit out of me while I'm just gill-filling her. It's a total rush. She doesn't have to beat my ass every time we have sex, but a couple of slaps would be great. I like slapping girls on the ass during sex.

The loudest sex I ever had was probably with Zap from American Gladiators, who I got together with a few times in the summer of 1995, when I was staying at Dwight's place in Newport Beach. We were two strong specimens going at it, and she could definitely hang with me physically. **One night we were having sex on Dwight's pool table, and the next morning he told me we sounded like a couple of dinosaurs going at it.**

A couple of times things have gotten too rough for my own

good, and I've broken my dick. You ask, "What's a broken dick?" If you've ever had one, or seen one, you know. I'll tell you this— it is not a pretty sight. The first time it happened I was up vacationing with some friends on my boat, a 43-foot Scarab, on Lake Texoma in Texas. I was with this very wild woman and we just tore each other up. It actually didn't happen on my boat, though there has been an unreal amount of sex on that craft. Everyone drinks and has a good time, and it's like you wake up and you've slept with someone you didn't even realize was on board the boat.

Anyway, back to the vessel that counts—the one between my legs. I had rented these two houseboats, both of them two stories high, and it was four o'clock in the morning and everybody was partying their asses off. A bunch of boats were tied up together in a row, and there were parties on all of them. We screwed so hard that as I was thrusting inside her, my dick bent against her pelvic bone and just broke. It swelled up to a very large size, turned purple and filled with blood—I guess it tore up a blood vessel, because I was pissing blood. About five or six days later it still was hurting me like shit. I was in New York for the MTV Awards, and late one night I decided to get it looked at. So Dwight and I ended up in an emergency room on the Upper East Side of Manhattan, in a waiting room full of people, including kids who were coming up and asking for autographs.

It was a total trip. People, including some of the kids, were asking me why I was there. What was I supposed to tell them? Dwight kept saying, "He doesn't feel well." Finally, they took me in to be examined, and what happened? Every doctor, nurse, intern, and medic in the whole hospital had to come in and grab my dick and check it out. Everybody got a nice look at Dennis Rodman's giant, bloody dick. I'm glad nobody came in and took a picture of it. It would've been all over the *National Enquirer.*

So finally, this doctor looks at me and says, "You have a contused penis." I said, "Come on, Doc. Do I have a broken dick or what?" He said, "In other words, yeah, your dick is broken." I said, "I thought so." There's nothing they can really do for you. You can't put a cast on it or anything. You basically can't have sex for a couple of weeks, and eventually it goes back to normal. But I think this is going to be a lingering injury for me, because it happened again a few months later, and I'm sure it won't be the last time.

Seven

Sleep Only When You're Dead

*W*hat a season I had in 1995–96, my first year with the Bulls. I averaged 5.5 points, 14.9 rebounds, 2.5 assists—and 4.3 hours of sleep per night.

No NBA player has ever partied the way I did that season and performed at such a high level. I went out almost every single night, and for me going out means eating dinner at 10 or 11 and then hitting the clubs and bars. In Chicago last call isn't until 5 A.M., and it's not uncommon for me to go the distance. And, of course, I often have female company once I do get to bed, which also tends to cut into my sleep.

The only problem is I almost always have to practice the next morning, often as early as 9 A.M. So, how do I manage to pull this off and stay faithful to my workout schedule? It's simple. **Something has to give, and for me that something is SLEEP.**

4.3 HOURS A NIGHT

Don't get me wrong. It's not that I have anything against sleep. It's just that there are so many other things I'd rather be doing.

They say you spend a third of your life sleeping. That's way too much, bro. There are so many things to experience and so little time. Every day I think of something new I'd like to try just once, maybe twice. I add those things to the list I keep in my head—a list that will never be satisfied. But as long as the list exists, each day is like an adventure, and there's always new ground to break. So many people get comfortable in a routine and surrender their quest for novelty and excitement, but not me. What I'm telling you is, Don't Sleep Through Life. Spend each and every waking hour ready to **SEE, SMELL, TOUCH, HEAR,** and **FEEL EVERYTHING YOU CAN.** And if it comes down to a choice between crashing and bashing, go for the latter every time. It's great to chase your dreams, but do it with your eyes open. If you snooze, you lose, and I don't plan to go to my grave a loser.

I'd rather party now and sleep later—much later. My motto is, **SLEEP ONLY WHEN YOU'RE DEAD.** What the hell else are you gonna do once you leave this earth? You'll have no choice but to sleep. I'll sleep when I die and have a big smile on my face.

Sometimes I'll catch a few winks while I'm sitting in my truck or hanging out at home or in a hotel room during the day. But it's not something I really think about, and it's rare that I feel tired when I'm out. It's mind over matter. I can usually get my body to behave the way I want it to. Sure, I might feel better rested if I went to bed earlier. But I'm having way too much fun to worry about sleep.

I'm having the time of my life. I'm living ten people's lives in one. In my first year in Chicago I had a fucking ball. It was one of the best years of my life. I was on the go, partying, doing all sorts of crazy shit. Some of it is so insane. It's like that Eagles song, **"Life in the Fast Lane."** That was me my first year with the Bulls, two times over. Everything, all the time. I was on the fucking Autobahn.

The last three years have been outrageous, and so far, my second year with the Bulls has been pretty wild—though not quite as out-of-control as the season before. I just don't seem to have that wild energy all the time. Maybe I'm getting old.

You know the Prince song that goes, "Tonight we're gonna party like it's 1999"? My attitude is, Why wait? When you've been through as much shit as I have, just being alive every day is worthy of celebration. So I try to treat every day like it's the turn of the century bash, because who knows how many more I'll have left.

Living life to the fullest gives me satisfaction. People tell you that you have to live a certain way, and that's so very wrong. Once you realize that life must be lived on your terms—that you must work to become the person you were born to be—it's a very liberating feeling. Life doesn't seem like so much of a struggle anymore. It can't be so limiting; it has to be about many different dimensions.

I learned all about living life to the fullest back in Bokchito,

Walk On The Wild Side

Oklahoma, when I lived with Bryne and his family. We used to hang out with this guy in his early forties named Don Taylor, who everyone called Duck. This guy lived for the moment like no one I've ever seen before or since. Duck had severe heart problems and was on prescription blood thinners. He knew he was living on borrowed time, so instead of listening to his doctor and cutting out alcohol, smoking, and fatty foods, he went the other way. The doctor once told him, "Duck, you need to quit drinking or you're gonna die." Duck looked at him long and hard and said, "Biggun, you tell me I can't get any pussy and can't get loaded—just cut my fuckin' throat right now."

So Duck did a lot of speed and drank a fifth of Lord Calvert whiskey every day, and when he died a few years ago there was no one who said, "If only he'd had more time," because the time he had was so amazing. He loved to gamble, and we'd always go over to his house and play poker well into the night. He was a lousy gambler, but the great thing was he didn't have to work. He had been working a construction job in California and fell off a scaffold—some say on purpose—and started drawing a permanent disability check. But he'd still end up broke at times. He lost both his pickup trucks in card games and this $1,000 smoker-cooker grill that you could hook behind a truck. Every so often he'd win the grill back, then lose it again. Bryne and Billy owned that thing for years.

Duck was hilarious. Many of my sayings—Biggun, Get Solid, No Shit—I got from him. Or he'd come up with lines like, **"I'm hell when I'm well but I'm never ill, *baby*,"** or

"ROUGH FUCK FOR A BUCK." I didn't drink back then, but I used to be amazed at the way Duck partied his ass off whether he had tons of cash or was broke as hell. And years later when I started drinking, I thought a lot about the way Duck went all out and how amazing it was to behold.

PARTYING IS NOT SOMETHING I TAKE LIGHTLY. To me it's the best way to get the most out of this life. It gives you a chance to meet interesting people and to create situations where unpredictable events can happen. If I stay home or hang out in a scene that is safe and doesn't change, I'm limiting my possibilities, and it's like I'm shutting down. If you don't go out you're not going to be tested or put in an unfamiliar position, and that means you probably won't gain anything from the night or learn much about yourself.

It's like the difference between watching a movie and going to a sporting event. The movie might be better than the sporting event, and it might move you, but it can only take you so far. You know about what time it will end and generally what it's about, and deep inside, you realize it's just people acting. But when you go to a sporting event there's a charge in the air that comes from people not really knowing what might happen, because the players are making it up as they go along. The game might suck, and chances are nothing totally amazing will take place. But you never know, and that's what makes it great.

When I talk about partying, I'm referring to much more than

going out and getting drunk—though, in my case, the two often go together. But I sometimes party without having anything to drink, and if I swore off alcohol today I'd still go out and rage and have a great time. It's all the mentality you bring to the table, and I'm someone who knows how to get high without anything at all. I've had friends of mine tell me I'm like an honorary acid-head or whatever because I party hard, my mind is open to trippy and unusual thoughts, and I'm totally immersed in the experience, whatever it may be at the moment.

TO ME THE KEY TO PARTYING IS IN THE **MENTAL PREPARATION.** THE WAY TO HAVE A GOOD TIME IS TO PREPARE YOURSELF TO HAVE A GOOD TIME THE DAY BEFORE. It's a visualization—you've got to visualize what's going to happen, when it's going to happen, how you're going to drink, how you're going to feel, if you're going to throw up . . . whatever it is, you put that in the mix. You have to prepare yourself for all those optical illusions that are going to hit you in the face. That doesn't mean you write the script beforehand and close yourself off to possibility. It just means you step into the zone of fun, because you have to get to that space before you can truly let go.

Another key to having a good time is finding the right place to go, and I seem to have a knack for that. It's sort of like my rebounding ability, the way I can sometimes just feel where the ball is going to bounce. In both cases, **IT COMES DOWN TO VIBES.** I can walk into a place and tell right away if the vibe is right for me.

What I'm looking for is a place where people don't look at you and judge you, a place where people are doing their own thing but also are curious about what's going on around. I like it when people don't give a fuck what you look like or who you are, and you can just let loose and have a good time. The worst is when I go somewhere that's not really that cool, but people act like they're having a great time just because I'm there. It's a bunch of bullshit, and I can spot it right away. I strongly believe you should **MAKE YOUR OWN FUN**, and when I see people who are relying on someone else to get their kicks, **MY ASSHOLE SENSOR GOES OFF.** I can tell when people's rubber balls are wound too fucking tight, and my reaction is to leave immediately.

When I'm in Chicago or Dallas or L.A. or a city I know well, it's easy to decide where to party. But if I'm in a place I'm not too familiar with, I usually just get into a car or cab and sort of go with the flow. I might end up at a 24-hour disco with nobody in there, but I'll go in and have a couple of drinks. Or I might start out at a taxi bar. A lot of times I'll go to an artsy part of town and just hang out—maybe at a clothing store or a tattoo parlor or a cafe. I'll talk to the people there, to find out what's going on, and go from there.

Sometimes when I don't want to be hassled, I'll go to gay bars or strip clubs. At gay bars, people definitely react to me, but they usually give me my space. ***GAY PEOPLE TEND TO UNDER-STAND WHAT IT'S LIKE TO HAVE EVERYONE POINTING AT THEM*** or talking about them as they walk by, and they can sense when to back off. Strip clubs are also cool that way, because two forces are at work: First, a lot of the people are too busy checking out the dancers and trying to get themselves off to worry about me. And secondly, many customers are self-conscious about being there, so they're trying to keep things low-key.

So, instead of going to a nightclub and getting hassled with a million questions, a lot of times I'll cool out at a cabaret. Obviously, that's not the only reason I go. Like most other guys, I like to sit back and enjoy the entertainment. To me, there's nothing sleazy about it at all. It's more up front than a dance club where everyone's trying to hit on each other. You know people want to see each other naked, and strip clubs cut to the chase. There are no strings attached, literally and figuratively. You can pay for a lap-dance, or you can just hang out and talk to a dancer.

Strip clubs perform a vital service for society. They're places where guys can go look at pretty girls and get away from their wives and girlfriends that are bitching at them all the time. If I was married and I was a sports figure I'd tell my wife, "Honey, I'm going to a strip joint. I have no choice." **IT BEATS STAY- ING HOME AND LOOKING AT FOUR WALLS AND JACKING OFF ALL THE TIME.** That gets a little old. But after you get back from a strip club, you're ready to rip your wife's clothes off and do her on the living room floor.

I also like going to clubs where it's dark and the music is loud and pulsating and it's packed with people and everyone is drinking and dancing and just going off. I can't exactly blend in to this type of scene, but it definitely helps me loosen my inhibitions, which is always a major goal when I go out partying. One of the best places I've found is Crobar, the one in Chicago with the cages and the bondage rack and the lesbian deejay named Psychobitch. I spent a lot of time at Crobar during the 95–96 season and I had my thirty-fifth birthday party there during the playoffs, which was pretty much the ultimate partying experience.

We had just beaten the New York Knicks to close out the series and advance to the Eastern Conference finals against the Orlando Magic. It was May 14, 1996, and it's a good bet that by the end of the night I had downed at least one shot for each of my thirty-five years. And I wasn't even the drunkest person there. **EDDIE VEDDER MIGHT HAVE BEEN;** one of my friends ended up having to carry him up to his hotel room. The next day Eddie said, "I think I had a really good time. Don't tell anybody." He's a pretty small guy as it is, it probably didn't help that he and I and some other friends went out for sushi after the game and downed about thirty-two bottles of sake before we even left for the party.

Crobar is almost always jam-packed, but on this night it was beyond jam-packed. The live music was incredible. Onstage with the blues-funk band Liquid Soul were Jeff Ament, my buddy from Pearl Jam, and big John Popper, the singer and harmonica player from Blues Traveler. Eddie didn't sing with the band, but he went onstage to lead the whole damn club in singing "Happy Birthday" to me. He and I sprayed the crowd with beers, and people threw their drinks right back at us until we were soaked. People were throwing up all over themselves, and they didn't give a damn.

Jeff was hysterical that night, talking to everybody, dancing on the bar. All these girls got up and danced together and started taking their clothes off, like they were Las Vegas showgirls. And then this one guy there was dressed up like a fairy, with wings and everything, and everyone was like, "Where the fuck did he come from?" **I gave the** FAIRY A BIG, WET KISS ON THE LIPS.

By the time the night was over, my friends—or at least the few who were still conscious—said I looked and sounded like Rocky Balboa. I was calling out for some girl, screaming blindly like Rocky did for Adrienne in the movies. Even in my obliterated condition, I felt like the heavyweight champion of the world.

The whole playoffs were like a blur to me.

You know how some players crank up their game once the regular season ends? I definitely took my game to the next level, on and off the court. The playoffs meant more friends bopping into town, and when those friends are people like Bryne or Cousin Al or some of the other insane people I know, that meant more drinking and less sleep. It was wild, but we took care of business on the court, winning fourteen of our first fifteen games, so nobody could say shit.

I was thinking things would be more mellow in 96–97, and I kept things relatively low-key during training camp and the exhibition season. But something clicked on the night of our home opener against the Philadelphia 76ers, and it was like, here we go again. After the game a bunch of us, including my crazy friend Billy from Dallas, went out to dinner and to this bar called the Drink, which was raging. Then we went to Crobar, and **FROM THE MOMENT I WALKED IN THERE I WAS LIKE A MAN POSSESSED.**

Everyone was screaming for me and grabbing me as I walked by, and this techno-house music was blaring away, just hypno-tizing people. The **MUSIC AND THE PANDEMONIUM just took hold of me,** and it was like this volcano of energy was building up inside my body. I had to explode, and before I knew what I was even doing I was climbing up into one of the cages above the dance floor. There were three hot women in skimpy leather outfits up there, and they were very happy to see me. *We started* **DRY-HUMPING** *each other and* **SIMULATING SEX** *while we danced* and people below were loving it, screaming for more. I took off my shirt and threw it down through the bars in the cage and danced with one of the women while the other two pretended to hump each other. SOON MY PANTS WERE DOWN TO MY KNEES and everyone was checking out my ass. When I got down from the cage people were reacting so outrageously to my performance that I got pushed into this corner by the edge of one of the bars and stayed there the rest of the night.

Walk On The Wild Side

People ask me if Crobar is the greatest place to party, but it can't be, because it's in the wrong city. Chicago is an amazing town, and if it wasn't for the butt-cold weather, it would be pretty damn close to perfect. Still, there's one city that will always kick every other place's ass when it comes to providing an uncontrollable party atmosphere, and that city is Las Vegas.

If you call the Mirage Casino and ask for me, they'll tell you one of two things: "One moment, please," or "Dennis isn't with us tonight." It's like my home away from home. I've been going there for years, and I used to be able to just go fucking ballistic. Now that I've become more famous over the last couple of years, it's a little more restrained, mostly because there are so many tourists watching me and trying to talk to me while I gamble or do whatever. It's like I'm being watched by thousands of eyes and being touched by millions of hands. It gets annoying, but I don't mind it that much, because so many people in Vegas are so freaky that in my head I can just blend in and exist as part of the crowd.

Vegas is the capital of the world for sex, money, drugs, and crime. And fun. **THE NAME OF THE CITY SHOULD BE F - U - N V E G A S .** It's a place where there are no boundaries. Anything goes, all night long. *IT'S ONE OF THE FEW PLACES THAT I CAN GO AND REALLY EXPRESS MYSELF THE WAY I WANT TO* without people looking at me all weird—except for the tourists, of course. You never know what kind of freaky scenes you'll be part of. Sometimes random freaks, people I don't even know, will call me at the Mirage and invite me to sex parties in the hotel. And if I'm not too busy, what the hell . . .

When I'm rolling into town, cruising down the crowded Strip, I get a rush you wouldn't believe. Part of it is the knowledge that anything can happen. Vegas is a place where you're always running into random people. It's probably one of the only places in the world where you can always find someone you know. Maybe you know them from ten years ago or twenty years ago or yesterday, but you'll always find people there.

Vegas is an incredible party town because people are not only wrapped up in sin, they're so up-front and excited about it. During the summer of '96 I had two of the greatest party nights ever, back-to-back. I was with two friends and we went, appropriately, to a bar called the Drink. Vince Neil from Mötley Crüe was there, and we started hanging out. He used to go out with Stacy, my ex-girlfriend, so at least we had that in common. We ended up going onstage together and singing, though all I could manage to blurt out was, "Yeah . . . yeah."

It was incredibly wild, but the next night topped it. We ended up practically starting a riot at a place called the Beach Club. We were ordering kamikazes by the bucket and my friend got so hammered he wanted to go home. I told him, "You work for me, bro. You're staying." I got up onstage again, this time with a seventies cover band called Boogie Nights. They gave me a big afro wig and I wore it while I grooved to songs like the Ojays' "Rollercoaster." At one point I took my shirt off and threw it into the crowd. Everyone lunged for it and a full-on fistfight broke out, and the cops had to come and break it up. Pretty soon everyone was taking off his or her shirt and throwing it, and I had to buy "Beach Club" T-shirts for a bunch of my friends.

Still, that was nothing compared to the dough I dropped about an hour later when I decided to buy beers for everyone in the club. While standing on the bar, I started grabbing cases, pulling out bottles and lofting them down into the crowd. Eventually they ran out of cold beers so I grabbed warm ones and tossed them down, too. **WE WENT THROUGH 130 CASES IN ALL, AND I RACKED UP A BAR TAB OF $8,000.** I don't remember much else from the night, except that at one point a young dude in a wheelchair fought his way up to the front of the bar and tried to get close to me. I walked up to him and talked to him about life and fate and we ended up exchanging T-shirts. Then we hugged and I noticed he was crying, and that's when I decided that life is precious and deserves to be celebrated.

You can see why I consider Vegas the world's premier party town. The greatest thing of all—of course—is the activity that makes Vegas Vegas: the gambling. I love to gamble, not so much because of the money but because of the thrill. That's why craps is my game. It's a social game, and the best moments come when you get on a table where that group vibe just blossoms. **WHEN MICHAEL JORDAN COMES TO THE MIRAGE,** they usually put him in a private room and he sits there playing blackjack all night, just him and a dealer. **CAN**

YOU IMAGINE ANYTHING MORE DULL? I could never do that, no matter how annoying it gets being touched while I'm playing craps. It's a game that requires concentration, and people are always breaking my focus. When they touch me, I jump. I'm trying to get into a zone—hell, the whole table is— and people come by and snap me out of my trance, and it sucks. What I try to do is make myself blind to what's going on around me and just focus on those dice.

One time I got interrupted at the black-jack table by Chevy Chase, of all people. He was tripping out on how many people I had with me and launched into a comedy routine right there. I didn't even know the guy, and he's capping on me for having an entourage and all sorts of shit. It was funny as hell, and I was laughing along with every-body else.

I'VE LOST A LOT OF MONEY PLAYING CRAPS, as much as **$35,000 IN ONE TRIP,** but I've had some good nights, too, and I'm not really worried about my cash flow when I'm down there on the casino floor. I'm much more moved by the rush than anything else. I love the idea that every time you put your money down there's a chance you'll win and a chance you'll lose—it could go either way, and how it turns out is a mystery. And the thing is, you lose so much more often than you win that it makes it that much more exciting when you do win.

I don't mind losing in Vegas. I'm not expecting to win, and I'm not stupid enough to think I can be the one to beat the odds.

Losing at craps is nothing like losing a basketball game. When you lose a game, your competitive juices are flowing, and you have pride on the line, and it hurts. At the craps table, it's a different kind of losing. You know that it comes down to chance, so you don't have to be competitive about it.

As for winning, that's just an incredible buzz. It's so rare that when it actually happens, you love it. It's what makes you come back to do it again. My winning bet—or at least the one I love to win with the most—is the Hard-10. That's why I wear No. 91 in Chicago—9 plus 1 is a Hard-10. **I CALL IT A HARD DICK,** because you definitely get that when you're out there throwing the dice and drinking your ass off, and especially if you're with the girl that you want to be with. Most of the time I walk around the Mirage with a **BIG SEMI** in my pants.

It's tempting to check into the Mirage and never leave, but I don't need to live in Vegas, because I can just go there whenever I'm in the mood. Besides, if I lived there it would probably kill me. I think the worst thing in the world would be if the NBA put a team in Vegas, because players wouldn't know how to control themselves. You'd have to have a very strong mind. I could probably do it, but it would be a major test.

I got a small taste of this during the 1996 preseason when we played an exhibition game in Vegas against the Utah Jazz. The team stayed at the Mirage, so you can imagine how that went. I was hoping Phil Jackson would let me sit out the game, so I could go nuts the night before, but it turned out I had to play. So I took care of business myself. I had already picked up one technical foul, and the game was running late, and I was worried we'd miss our 11 P.M. dinner reservations at Mikado's, a restaurant inside the Mirage. So, as it happened, I picked up another "T" and was able to get the hell of there and start my party night right on time.

It was our typical crazy Vegas night, with the usual crowd of lunatics. We were hoping **MIKE TYSON,** who lives in Vegas, would come to dinner with us, but he said he couldn't because **IT WAS PAST HIS BEDTIME.** Mike Tyson? Bedtime?

Whatever, bro.

Eight

Just Say, "Fuck No"

THEY OUGHT TO STICK ME RIGHT IN THE MIDDLE OF ONE OF THOSE ANTIDRUG CAMPAIGNS. I'm like another former Motor City Madman, Ted Nugent—I'm the guy you'd least expect not to do drugs. I could see it now, a commercial with me and Nancy Reagan, with Ted rocking out in the background. Nancy would be in a leather miniskirt and low-cut blouse with pumps, and I'd be wearing a G-string with a jungle design and a sequined halter top.

Nancy: If someone offers you drugs, Just Say "No."

Me: That's right, bro, TELL 'EM TO KISS YOUR HAIRY BLACK ASS.

Nancy: Say no to drugs, and you'll grow up to be big, tall, and healthy like my friend Dennis.

Me: I have a great time without acid, weed, shrooms, junk, crack, or any of that other shit. If anyone tries to get you to do any of that stuff, **JUST SAY, "FUCK NO."**

Nancy: Yes, because drugs are bad.

Ted: They'll get you in a stranglehold, baby, you'd best get out of their way . . .

A lot of people have trouble believing that I don't do drugs, especially when they see the way I live my live. But it's true—I don't do drugs and I never have. **I DIDN'T INHALE, AND I DIDN'T EXHALE.**

Does that mean I never will do drugs? Who knows. I might want to smoke a big, fat joint sometime, just to see what it's like. Then again I've done pretty well without the evil weed, so why fuck with a good thing? I know this: If I ever do try something illegal like pot, I'll wait until I'm done playing basketball. I'm not gonna give David Stern and his boys at the NBA office the satisfaction of nailing me for something like that.

Here's what I'd really like to tell kids. Yeah, I'd do drugs—if I was a stupid, crazy, jiving son-of-a-bitch. Yeah, I would do it, just because everybody else is doing it, if I wanted to throw my life away. **BUT YOU CAN BE BETTER THAN THAT. IT'S YOUR CHOICE.**

Looking back, it's pretty amazing that I didn't try drugs at least once when I was a kid. Shit, by the time I was eighteen and living in the projects, everyone I knew was at least smoking pot. My sister, Debra, used to light up joints in the house—she didn't care. She never offered it to me, though, because she knew how I felt about the issue. I had decided early on that drugs are bad. I really don't know how I came to think that. Nobody ever gave me any antidrug lectures, or at least any that I took seriously. I don't think most kids in the projects listen to that shit, anyway.

So why haven't I tried drugs? That's a strange, strange question to ask me. I've been around them all my life and I'm still around them—it's even worse today. I've got friends that do various drugs all the time, but they know I'm against it and they try not to put it in my face. One thing about drugs is it seems like they can just grab ahold of you and make you into something you're not. I know alcohol can do that, too, but for some reason I don't feel out of control when I'm drunk. You have to be responsible and know your limits. I have a pretty high tolerance, and I've been there before. I still have a sense of awareness of what's going on when I'm drunk, and if I have to snap out of it—like if I have to deal with a cop or something—I can. But ***people on drugs are in la-la land.***

Alcohol loosens your inhibitions and makes you do some pretty ridiculous things. But if you've been drunk enough times, there's a kind of buffer that cushions you from the unexpected. When I'm drunk, I'm not gonna jump off the top of Sears Tower because I think I can fly. I'm not gonna start scratching the skin off my face. I might end up face down on the toilet, but I won't be in a straitjacket. With drugs, you just never know. And while I'm curious about the experiences certain drugs might provide for me, I'M CONFIDENT IN MY MIND'S ABILITY TO TAKE ME TO SOME PRETTY FAR-OUT PLACES WHEN I'M NOT HIGH.

I'm pretty aware of the ways in which alcohol affects me, and I feel like I can control it in a way in which I won't endanger myself or anybody else. But with drugs, people can get really out of control. There are a lot of levels you can go to, and you can get addicted to all kinds of drugs. You can get in a dangerous zone where you don't know what day it is. From what I've seen and heard, it's like you're all of a sudden in a different area code, and you're saying, "How the hell did I get here?"

I didn't start drinking until I was in my late twenties, except maybe for a couple of beers back in college that gave me a slight buzz, but that was it. When all my friends were drinking OE8s in the projects—that's what they call Old English 800 Malt Liquor—I was staying clean and sober. When I thought I could handle it, I decided to explore. Drinking gives you a sense of being totally lost, and within the moment and the buzz, you're just very content with what's going on right then. It loosens you up and loosens up the people around you, and it can lead to some funny and crazy shit. I love being punch-drunk the next morning, sitting around with my friends and remembering the madness from the night before.

Then again, **DRINKING is not for everyone.** Some people simply can't handle it, and when they're drunk it's not a pretty sight. It's a decision everyone has to make, and my decision right

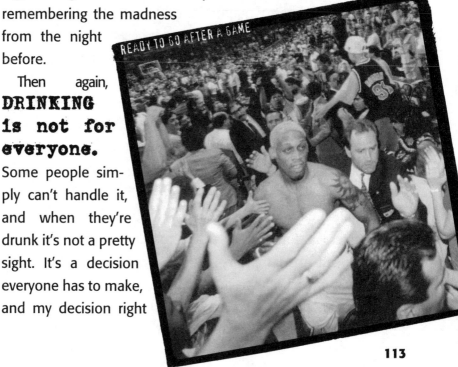

READY TO GO AFTER A GAME

now is to drink socially. But a few of my friends don't drink at all, and I respect them for that.

Now for the big question: How do I do it? **HOW CAN A THIRTY-FIVE-YEAR-OLD MAN DRINK HIS ASS OFF, SLEEP VERY LITTLE AND PLAY IN THE NBA—AND STILL BE THE BEST-CONDITIONED GUY ON THE COURT?**

To give you the God-honest truth, bro, I don't really even know. Part of it is that I work out like a fiend. I go to the gym twice a day, no matter what, and my workouts are comprehensive—I work on many different muscles and I do a lot of cardiovascular shit. And then I'll spend a long time in the sauna, which is great for hangovers. The bottom line is I'll do what I have to do until my body gets whipped into shape. If that means going wild on the StairMaster before a game or working out for an hour when the game ends, so be it. I have to get that poison out of my body, no matter what it takes.

IT'S MIND OVER MATTER. I know that if I don't get up and overcome the shitty feeling I have, then I'll end up in somebody's wasteland. So I hypnotize myself to the point where I can deal with the pain and the nausea. I motivate myself to get my ass up and go work out so that I can cleanse my body and feel good again.

Even after I'm done playing basketball, I'm still going to get up and work out every morning. I've always told myself I'm not gonna be a typical athlete that retires and gets fat. I'm always going to be in shape, I'll make sure of that. It's so important to my mental health. If you let your body slip, you feel shitty about yourself, like you're a worthless tub of lard. But after a workout I feel great, even when I have a hangover.

So, as you can see, I've developed this successful system that allows me to work hard and play hard. The only time there's a problem is when the lines get blurred. That has happened a couple of times, and they've been pretty scary.

The all-time* CRAZIEST STUNT *was when I played in an NBA game while I was still drunk from the night before. It happened in Phoenix in March of 1994, when I was with the San Antonio Spurs. The night before our game against the Suns, Bryne Rich and I and a couple of women went out and got bombed. Charles Barkley, who played for the Suns at the time, was at the bar, too, but he didn't really get too crazy and went home a long time before us. We were doing these disgusting "Sex on the Beach" shots, a sweet mixture of various liquors, and the party sort of continued into the wee morning hours. **I barely slept,** and when I got up to go to the shootaround, EVERYONE ON MY TEAM WAS LIKE, "GOD DAMN, YOU STINK LIKE A BREWERY." I had the worst hangover in the world, and I was just feeling like shit, so **I brilliantly tried to make myself feel better by having a couple of drinks during the day.**

When I got to the arena I was still **BUZZING.** I had a massive headache, and my stomach was pretty weak. What the hell was I gonna do? I thought about making up some lame-ass excuse and scratching myself from the lineup, but that seemed like a pretty gutless thing to do. Besides, it would have been like admitting that alcohol had gotten the best of me.

I thought about Dock Ellis, that crazy bastard who used to pitch for the Pittsburgh Pirates and the Texas Rangers in the seventies. This guy was nuts, and one day when it wasn't his turn to pitch he went out with some people and ended up taking LSD. He had a game that night, and he figured he'd just sit in the bullpen and trip. But the guy who was supposed to pitch got hurt at the last minute, and the manager said, "Ellis, you're pitching." So he had no choice but to go out there, and what happens? The guy throws a no-hitter.

Not only was this the greatest feat in sports history, **it was the GREATEST FEAT in DRUG HISTORY.** It might have been the greatest feat in history, period. I figure he walked out there, saw about three gloves and four home-plate umpires, and said to himself, "OK, the first guy who gets a hit off me, I'm out of here."

Thinking about that made me realize that it always comes down to mind over matter, so I decided to go balls out and try to play with a big heat on. I wasn't falling down drunk or anything, but it's a good thing nobody gave me a breathalyzer, because I definitely would've been over the legal driving limit. Right before the game started I put my head in my hands and thought to myself,

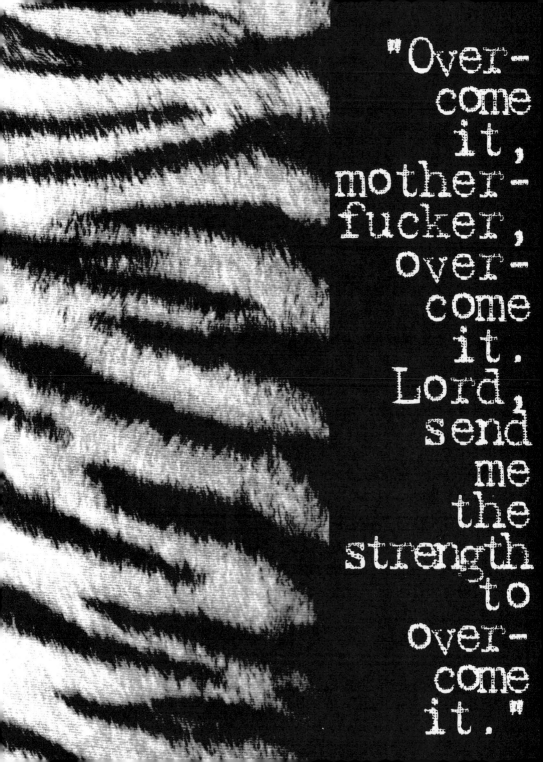
"Over-
come
it,
mother-
fucker,
over-
come
it.
Lord,
send
me
the
strength
to
over-
come
it."

Then we went out there to start the game, and some problems cropped up immediately. First off, the opening whistle sent a sharp pain through my head. The fans were screaming and the music was blasting and the horn was blaring and there was nothing I could do—I just had to make it through. Then there was the matter of the lights. They were too bright, and hurt my eyes. Barkley looked at me and said, "What

CHARLES BARKLEY SPLIT MY LIP

the fuck did you do last night?" He knew damn well what I did. I told him, "Well, I guess I had a little too much to drink." He laughed and said, "Hey, they can't keep us from going out and having a good time. We're allowed that right." Then, on the next play, he elbowed me right in the lip, and I had to leave the game for a couple of minutes.

It was a struggle, and **I felt like shit most of the game.** But the more I played, the better it got. And it turned out I was able to overcome—I had a pretty damn good game. I had 13 points and 15 rebounds, and we were winning by so much that I sat out the entire fourth quarter. It wasn't quite Dock Ellis, but it wasn't too shabby.

After hearing a story like this, **SOME PEOPLE** *automatically believe I have a drinking problem.* It's possible; I'm not an expert on the subject, so who am I to say? But I am an expert on the subject of me, and I don't see my drinking as a real issue. It's something I do, but it doesn't define me. `I don't do stupid shit LIKE START FIGHTS or BEAT UP WOMEN`, and **I DON'T DRINK AND DRIVE.** I'll take a limo or a cab or get someone else to drive me. Obviously there have been a few times in my life where I've broken that rule—most of us have at one time or another. But generally, my attitude is *DON'T DRIVE DRUNK, BECAUSE IT'S JUST NOT WORTH IT.* When you do that, you make drinking about more than yourself. You make your drinking a problem for other people.

Nine

Live
Loud
and
Proud

*i*n the summer of 1996, shortly after the completion of the NBA Finals, I took a quick vacation to Maui with Eddie Vedder. This trip really was a trip, because Eddie and I are so much alike, yet we're so different. Eddie tries to hide from his fame, while I flaunt mine, but **WE'RE BOTH STRUGGLING TO BE TRUE TO OURSELVES AND TO HAVE A GREAT TIME.** And on one Hawaiian party night I'll never forget, it all came together in a totally unexpected way.

We had been out messing around on motorcycles and having

ME, DWIGHT, & EDDIE: THE BEST VACATION I EVER HAD.

some fun, and we ended up at a bar called Moose McGillicudy's in Lahaina. There were some people with us, including Eddie's younger brother, Dwight Manley, and my friend Erika, and we were just sitting there having some wine while this bar band was rocking out in the background. All of a sudden, the band started playing "Go," the first song on "Vs.", which is Pearl Jam's second album. It's an awesome, fast-paced song that's really hard to sing, and Eddie got this look on his face and said, **"They're not singing it right."** I could see what he was thinking, but I didn't believe it would actually happen. He looked straight into my eyes and said, "Should we?" I sort of shrugged and said, "That's up to you, bro." He stood up and said, "OK, let's do it," and we walked right up to the stage.

Now, imagine you're some bar band doing a Pearl Jam cover and Eddie Vedder appears onstage. You're gonna piss your pants, and that's exactly what they did. The singer almost died, bro. Everybody in the band was tripping. Eddie grabbed the microphone and started singing, and I was sort of dancing next to him, and the place went absolutely nuts. The band musicians totally raised their game, just like a bunch of playground hoopsters would if Michael Jordan and Larry Bird showed up to play. They started playing harder and better than even they knew they could, and ***Eddie was getting totally into it,*** **SCREAMING** *and* **HOLLERING.** And think of the people in the bar. They were like, "This can't be happening." The dance floor was in a frenzy, and the amazing thing was that word spread like herpes. All of a sudden hundreds of people were streaming in from the street—upstairs, downstairs, every-where—and it was packed. People were jumping up and down and going nuts.

The band ended up playing two more Pearl Jam songs, and Eddie sang his lungs out. Then he and I went to our table and ordered another drink. What made the moment truly amazing was that it was so unlike Eddie to throw himself out there like that. He's usually the guy trying to sneak around in the shadows and avoid getting noticed.

Eddie exists in his own solar system, and I dig that. He doesn't want things to change. He wants things to be the way they were before he was famous. And he gets frustrated, because it can't be that way anymore for him. Everywhere he goes people just freak out, and that's understandable—the guy has moved a lot of people to feel emotions they weren't even in touch with before they heard his music.

We talk about this fame issue all the time. People hang all over me when we're out together, and Eddie obviously gets his share of attention, but he can't deal with it. So he doesn't deal with it. He lies low. When he does go somewhere crowded, he's able to keep a low profile—literally—because he's so small. But when he sees the way I approach things, just going out in public and throwing myself out there, it freaks him out. He says, "It's amazing how you deal with all this." He wonders how the hell I do it.

Walk On The Wild Side

I tell Eddie he should give in and do what I do, that he might as well just accept it. ***"JUST DEAL WITH IT, BRO,"*** I always say to him. At least he can go out and disguise himself. At his concerts, long before the band goes on, he's constantly doing stuff like putting on masks or dressing up like a clown and wading into the audience. Sometimes he'll pass out leaflets just to see how people react. At the show in Augusta, Maine, that I went to in September of 1996—the one where I ended up bringing him a glass of red wine onstage—he put on this silver suit and a mask and cruised around through the crowd, and then he went up and sang with the opening band, and nobody knew who he was.

Can you imagine what would happen if I tried to pull some shit like that? There's no way I can disguise myself: I'm 6-8, there are tattoos all over my body and my hair is always some bright color. It would be tempting to try to conceal my identity, but even if I could I don't think I would, because it goes against my basic philoso-phy: **LIVE**

SHOWING MY FACE IN PUBLIC

LOUD AND PROUD—And Be Comfortable In A Crowd.

What I'm saying is that nobody should be afraid to mingle, even if doing so causes discomfort. *If you're gay or short or funny-looking or extremely shy or whatever, you still need to go outside of your shell and live your life, because every moment on this earth is precious, and there's no time to hide away.* It's important that no matter who you are you don't let the assholes who are making you uncomfortable get the upper hand. If you're too scared to go out and face them, then they've won, and they'll go right on hurting people. I know, because I USED TO BE A SHY, FUNNY-LOOKING NOBODY who spent his life avoiding those assholes. Even when I got tall and became a pro basketball player, it still took years before I was comfortable enough to show the world the real me. Instead, I was showing people the guy I thought everyone wanted me to be.

I learned my lesson the hard way, and I hope other people in the same situation don't have to go through all the pain and bullshit that I did. I spent so many years feeling shitty about myself because I KNEW IN MY HEART I WAS LIVING A LIE. Man, I wish I could have those years back. I've blocked out a lot of the memories, and now it seems fuzzy, like when you wake up from a nightmare. You think, "Wow, I've been asleep all this time, and I just woke up and I don't know where the hell I am." It's hard to grasp onto the moments from my past life, and I usually don't even try, because I've moved on.

NO MATTER WHO YOU ARE, YOU SHOULD BE PROUD OF IT, and you should show that pride in the way you carry yourself in public. If other people are bothered by that then it's their problem, not yours. So many celebrities try to hide from their fame, and that's a strange thing. Most people in the public eye got to that point because they have a flair for performance and a desire to be noticed. I admit it—I like being a star. I don't need it, but I like it, so I go with it. Besides, I figure if you can't hide, you might as well go the opposite route and just throw yourself into the mix. Interacting with regular people in public places makes me feel alive and electric. In the past year and a half my fame has gotten out of hand, and it's difficult even for some of my friends to hang out with me. It's like I created a monster that keeps stomping through life, and there's no use keeping him under lock and key. If the monster wants to dance, you better clear out some space on the dance floor.

The whole idea of being a celebrity is kind of freaky to begin with, and the best way to deal with it is to have some fun. That's why I act the way I do on the basketball court—because it's a show, and if everyone's watching, I might as well be an actor. *I'M AN EXHIBITIONIST AT HEART,* and I used to worry that nobody would ever give a damn about me or notice anything I did. Now I have an audience larger than I ever dreamed possible, and I intend to make the most of it.

FANS' TOP 10 STUPIDEST STATEMENTS (And My Responses)

Fans are the greatest, but every time, I'm out in public, people approach me as if they're my long-lost relatives. Sometimes they say some utterly ridiculous things.

10. **Remember me? I played craps with you in Vegas.** (Yeah, you and the rest of the world.)

9. **Can you get me a jersey?** (No problem, they only cost $600, and I happen to have several with me right now.)

8. **Where's Jack Haley?** (What am I, his wife?)

7. **You know, I think you're the best player in the world.** (Yeah, right.)

6. **Do you mind if I take a picture of you?** (Of course I do, but even if I say yes I mind you'll take it anyway. Don't ask, just take.)

5. **What are you doing at this club?** (The same thing you are, obviously.)

4. **Do you know Michael Jordan?** (Uh, yeah.)

3. **Hey Dennis, where's Madonna?** (Probably out somewhere getting asked where I am.)

2. **Did you really head-butt that ref?** (No, that was a computer-enhanced videotape.)

1. **I hate to bother you, BUT ...** (If you hate to bother me, then why are you doing it?)

On the basketball court, I have a million ideas of how to spice up the show. When I joined the Bulls and I couldn't wear No. 10 because it was retired—Bob (Butterbean) Love, one of their great forwards from the seventies, used to have it—I WANTED TO WEAR NO. 69. But the Bulls wouldn't let me do that. Maybe they were still shell-shocked from that time a few years back when **Horace Grant posed in a Jacuzzi with a bunch of topless women** in one of those explicit men's magazines. The cool thing is that when I was a free agent after the '96 season I talked to the Los Angeles Lakers about signing with them, and Jerry West, their general manager (and also one of the greatest players of all time), thought the whole thing was funny as shit. So he had a gold No. 69 Lakers jersey made with my name on it. The Lakers ended up spending all their salary-cap money on Shaquille O'Neal, and I re-signed with the Bulls, but I kept the jersey. A few weeks later Eddie Vedder saw it and thought it was incredibly cool, so I gave it to him, and now I think he has it hanging in his house in Seattle.

I'd like to paint my face in Day-Glo colors and play in a game like that. I think it would be wild if the whole Bulls team came out for one game with all of our hair dyed the same color. Well, maybe Michael would still be bald, but the rest of us could do it, even Phil Jackson. People would just freak out. I'd love to go out there all made up like a woman. And, as I've said before, I hope to get naked on the court during my last NBA game.

As for my life off the court, there are even more opportunities for me to be outrageous. When I dress up in drag or ride a Harley into a bookstore, people seem to get a charge out of it, so why the hell not? I'm intrigued by the idea of public theater, and the ultimate example of that for me, so far, was the mock wedding I staged in midtown Manhattan in August of '96.

Everyone saw the wedding as a publicity stunt, and with good reason: I didn't actually get married,

HERE COMES THE BRIDE ALL DRESSED IN DRAG

and I ended up doing a book-signing while wearing a bridal dress and veil. But let's think about this: Do I really need the publicity? Staging the wedding—and announcing it the previous night on *The Late Show With David Letterman*—was definitely a calculated ploy. But the reasons behind it were not what you might think.

I DID IT FOR THE RUSH, AND BECAUSE IT WAS A CHANCE FOR ME SYMBOLICALLY TO MARRY MY FANS. I have many different sides to my personality—some masculine, some feminine—and the ceremony brought all of them together and allowed me to feel whole.

Also, I got married because I knew it would cause a commotion, and I wanted to see the way people would react. And believe me, they tripped. Getting dressed up for the big day was an experience in itself. I had some of the world's best makeup artists working on me, and the room was just packed with people. They got me into my dress, and I had the whole package except for the shoes—I just wore white socks. What would have really taken the cake would've been if they put me in a sexy negligee, but I wasn't complaining. When I saw what they had done to me, I couldn't believe it. **THEY ACTUALLY MADE ME LOOK LIKE A PRETTY ATTRACTIVE CHICK.**

First we took a bus, we got into a carriage a couple of blocks away from Rockefeller Center, where we held the ceremony. It was me, Dwight, my bodyguards, and my bridesmaids, who were good-looking women in tuxedos. As we rode in the carriage, people around us were just screaming and going nuts. Traffic stopped, and I felt like Princess Di or something.

So laugh at the wedding all you want. Just realize that **for me, it was a SERIOUS, SINCERE, and SPE-CIAL EXPERIENCE.** I was so moved by it that I kept a diary. Here is some of what I wrote:

This land is for the few and far between, only open to those who have let their mind be free . . . Flew in from New York City after having a day of crazy-ass people screaming for a WEDDING. Wondering if the bride would come <u>out</u> . . . With God, white clouds of love and tears of joy, the bride appears upon a sea of silence. She steps softly toward her moment of glory. With each step she hears herself wondering aloud: **"What the FUCK am I doing? I'm not a woman, I'M A MAN THAT WANTED TO FEEL SOFT AND BEAUTIFUL AND DESIR-ABLE TO <u>MEN</u> and women.** It's hard to please both kinds, but the more I walk toward my flock, I feel that <u>vibe</u> take over my body from head to toe. Instead of walking cautiously I walk with pride and open eyes to what my mind has pictured for so long. Walk, Mrs. Rodman, you look good, you feel good. The sky has cleared . . . I always want to be what my mind really believes in; it doesn't hurt to cut pieces of life out of its book of <u>function</u>. *As individuals we desire a lot from life, BUT LIFE DOESN'T PLAY FAIR.* **NEITHER DO I.**

Looking back, I wish I would've done it better. I wish it had been in a tropical place, somewhere unique. I would've made a video to go along with it, one that would have shown all the trials and tribulations and the workouts and the makeup and all the preparation—everything that got me to this place. It would have had a theme song, sort of like "Come Fly With Me," but I would have used Pearl Jam: ". . . can't find a better man."

So it's possible I'll have another wedding, or maybe I'll give birth. Or, possibly, I'll stage my own funeral. A lot of famous people have talked about doing that—Jim Morrison and 2Pac, for example—but as far as I know, no one has ever pulled it off and lived to brag about it. Sometimes when things get hectic the idea of checking out sounds appealing, but it goes against my nature. If you go incognito, then you stop living life the way you want to live it. I can't do that. I've got to play, not sneak around in the rafters.

Life is fleeting, and when I think about all the stuff that could have messed me up, I'm blown away that I'm even here. Life is a wild scene, and I've got to be in it, man. I want to enjoy it. I mean, you could take all your friends, maybe the six people closest to you, and say, "Fuck it" and put them all in a little compound and just have a good time. But it doesn't work like that. It would get old, and things would get stagnant. ***It's important to get out there and Feel The* HEART-BEAT OF LIFE,** enjoy the festivities.

For me, one cool way to do that is to get inside other people, whether they're real or make-believe. That's why I enjoy acting. It's a chance to visualize realities different from your own, and to me that's a very natural process. You wake up and look in the mirror and put on makeup and go act—just like everyday life.

If you think about it, we're all performers. People perform every day of their lives. At work, they're playing various roles— boss, manager, secretary, whatever. **Wherever you work, YOU'VE GOT TO ACT LIKE YOU'RE HAPPY TO BE THERE, even though in the back of your mind you know it's bullshit.** Or think of it this way: right now, no matter what time of day it is, millions of people are fucking each other. What they're doing is performing an act, though in most cases it's a private performance.

Walk On The Wild Side

A few hours after my wedding in Manhattan, I got on a plane for Europe—just as I did after my wedding at the Chapel of the Bells in Lake Tahoe—and took on my first major acting challenge. There had been a few token roles before, like in the basketball movie *Eddie* or the sitcom *Third Rock from the Sun*, but in those situations I was playing myself and barely had any lines. This was a whole different league. We were in Arles, France, near the Riviera, filming *Double Team*, a movie starring Jean-Claude Van Damme, Mickey Rourke . . . and *moi*.

We had shot some scenes in Rome the previous month, and now we were in France for the hardest stretch of filming. We often worked into the night and slept till noon—perfect for my body clock, but that made partying a tough proposition. We only had a couple of big party nights, and the first one was the best. We were all at this restaurant in Arles, and right when we were about to get started, Mickey Rourke stood up and made a toast. "Most times I don't like socializing with people I'm working with," he said, "because actors are a bunch of fucking cunts. But I really like all of you, and I respect you, so let's go for it." When I heard that, I said to myself, "I love this guy." **HE'S SO STRAIGHT-OUT, SO UNAFRAID TO TELL PEOPLE THE WAY HE FEELS,** THAT YOU HAVE TO RESPECT HIM. He likes to party, he likes to enjoy life, and he likes to be himself, and that's the beauty of it.

Mickey was cool. He was going through some tough times in his marriage, and we talked a lot, 'cause I could definitely relate. One day I was hanging out in the trailer with my friend Stacy and we were just goofing around, bouncing it up and down and rocking it back and forth. I guess Mickey walked by and thought we were doing the wild thing, and that got him all excited. That night when we were shooting Mickey came up to me and said, "Yo, way to go." and we started laughing. I also liked Van Damme a lot. He's a sensitive guy who helped me out and made me feel comfortable.

I played an international weapons specialist named Yaz who helps Van Damme pull off some amazing shit. It was a lot of work, but I felt really comfortable in front of the camera. I like being on camera, because I don't feel any pressure. Some people freak out in front of the camera, but to me it doesn't seem threatening at all. I mean, ***IT'S EASIER TO BE ON CAMERA THAN TO FACE THE SHIT IN EVERY-DAY LIFE.*** It's just you and the camera, instead of people coming at you all the time giving you all this duress and stress.

So much of acting comes down to visualization, and I do that anyway. I analyze who this character is, I visualize being him and I project it. Then I become that character for a while. It goes back to what's in my head, and my job is to bring that picture to real life, that's all. Turn the switch, just like real life.

There are so many roles I'd like to play. I'd like to play a multifaceted character, someone who is good and evil. I can be anything you want me to be.

To me, acting and reality are intertwined, and that's how my MTV series, *Rodman World Tour*, is sort of set up. They gave me this old tour bus of Waylon Jennings's—a fellow Dallas Cowboys

HANGING OUT WITH JENNY MCCARTHY

fan—painted it for me and let me cruise around recruiting cool people like Ben Stiller or Whoopi Goldberg. I act out some of my fantasies. Tommy Lee teaches me how to play drums. I wish I had more time to devote to the show. I like the idea of living my life with cameras rolling, because if you stay with me long enough, you're going to capture some outrageous moments.

So, like the rest of the world, I guess I want to be a star. But one thing I will never, ever be is a Starfucker. Yes, I know what you're thinking: Wasn't I the guy who went out with Madonna and told the whole world about it? Yes, that was me, and **the whole thing was a fiasco.** I enjoyed Madonna's company, and I'm glad we got to hang out, but the relationship was incredibly difficult. A lot of mistakes were made in terms of what was publicized, and I wouldn't want to go out with any-body famous again.

Madonna got mad because she sent me some faxes and a friend of mine at the time who was living in my house in San Antonio took them and sold them to *Hard Copy*. She seems to think that I was the one who sold them: Come on, I would never do that. **If I needed money that badly, there are about a million other ways I'd rather go about getting it.** I told the guy who sold her faxes I would never do anything like that, and I got pissed off, and we're not friends anymore. Anyone who's really a friend would never do some-thing that lame. My friends know that if they need money that badly, they should just ask me.

Looking back, I probably shouldn't have been so open about my experiences with Madonna. Apparently it really hurt her. So I'll say it now: **MADONNA, I'M SORRY IF I CAUSED YOU ANY GRIEF. As we say on the basketball court, MY BAD.**

That said, how in the world can **Madonna get all pissed off at me** for revealing inti-mate details about our sex life? **WE'RE NOT EXACTLY TALKING ABOUT THE VIRGIN MARY HERE.** This is the woman who plays with herself in videos and puts out a book in which she is topless—with a dog. All that stuff is cool by me, but don't try getting all pure and holy on me all of a sudden. Of all the people to get paranoid about her image,

Madonna should be the last one. It would be like Wilt Chamberlain getting uptight because some woman talked about having a one-nighter with him.

I NEVER SAID ANYTHING BAD ABOUT MADONNA. I JUST TOLD THE TRUTH. I never said she's a bitch or a whore, and I never will, because I don't think she is. She needs to let stuff like this go. She's so big, this shouldn't even be touching her. She's one of the biggest stars of the twentieth century, maybe ever, so this shouldn't even be worth her energy, especially now that she has the baby.

At some point I'll probably talk to her again, and I think we'll be able to get past all this bullshit. I won't even bring it up. People have said a lot of crazy things about her and she just plays it off and goes about her business, and that's how it should be.

But would I date her again, or any other celebrity? Schnay. There's no way in hell I could do that, because it's hard enough trying to find a woman who isn't caught up in the whole celebrity thing, who is able to deal with the madness that goes along with dating me. If she's also a celebrity, that makes it even worse.

That doesn't mean I don't like hanging out with famous women in a casual way. *I went on a date with* **ROBIN QUIVERS** of the Howard Stern show because I found her incredibly interesting, and when we were on the radio together I guess I thought she was pretty wild. *She is a* **NICE, BIG-BUSTED WOMAN** *who's a very*

COOL CAT, A COOL PUSSYCAT. Our date was mellow: we just hung out and had some friends over, and at the end of the night I kissed her on the lips, and that was it.

I've also been out with **CINDY CRAWFORD** A COUPLE OF TIMES. We met last summer in Seattle during the NBA Finals. She was interviewing me for MTV's *House of Style*, and she had me trying on all these funky bathing suits. The highlight was when I put on a G-string. *HER MOUTH GOT ALL WIDE AND SHE LOOKED TOTALLY AMAZED WHEN SHE SAW* **MY BIG BULGE.** I told her, **"DON'T WORRY—***THERE'S A MONSTER IN MY PANTS, BUT IT'S JUST GETTING READY TO DANCE."* She cracked up. We went out that night, and I've seen her since then, but we're just friends. I wouldn't try to put the moves on her, because she's not that kind of girl. She's a nice midwestern girl with a lot of integrity, and she's very cool to hang out with.

ANOTHER CELEBRITY I GOT TO KNOW IN THE SUMMER OF '96 WAS TONI BRAXTON. We met at the MTV awards in New York. Someone had hooked me up with this Russian supermodel from the Guess Jeans ad campaign. But the model didn't have much to say, and I was in one of my shy moods. So even though I was sitting next to this model, I ended up talking to Toni, who was one row behind us. I finally asked the model to hold my coat and I cruised back and took the seat next to Toni. After the show we went to this party for Alannis Morissette, the singer who has this song called "Ironic" that lists a bunch of things—rain on your wedding day,

fly in your chardonnay—that aren't ironic at all. Maybe she was trying to create the ultimate irony, but I think she probably just doesn't understand the meaning of the word. Anyway, we were at this party and the model sat on one side of me and Toni sat on the other, and I spent the whole time talking to Toni. Then we went back to my limo and up to her hotel room, and we hung out till 6 A.M. At the end of the night, I just shook her hand and said, "Nice to meet you." She left her wallet and her watch in my limo and I had to meet her the next night to return them. Everyone thinks we must have been doing the wild thing that first night, but I swear all we did was talk. That's the wildest thing about having such a crazy image—even when you play it mellow, people give you credit for taking it to the limit. I've slept with Toni Braxton in my mind, like I have with a lot of people, but I swear all we were doing was talking about life. `We flapped our mouths all night long, but we didn't swap any spit.`

The crazy thing about Toni Braxton is she played a major role in the 1995–96 NBA season. Two of the stars of the Dallas Mavericks, Jason Kidd and Jimmy Jackson, got to know her a little bit and started competing for her affection. Neither got very far, but the way I've heard the story, they ended up having this stupidass feud, to the point where, supposedly, neither would pass the ball to the other one. That has to be the lamest thing I've ever heard of in sports. Maybe they wanted her because she's a star, and maybe they thought she has something good between her legs. But ***NO PUSSY IN THE WORLD IS WORTH DESTROYING A TEAM FOR.*** If something like that had happened when I was on the Detroit Pistons during our glory years, Isiah Thomas or Bill Laimbeer or Rick Mahorn would have straightened that shit out in a hurry. But today's players are different. **THEY ARE MUCH LESS COMMITTED TO WINNING THAN THEY USED TO BE.**

I DON'T TREAT FAMOUS PEOPLE ANY DIF-FERENTLY THAN I TREAT ANYONE ELSE I meet. It's other famous people who are always coming up to me, which is fine, but I don't get off on it. I've had rappers, comedians, actors, musicians approach me, partly because I'm an athlete, and partly because I'm so out there, they want to find out what makes me tick. But I'm usually not that interested in them. **Most STARS are sort of predictable.** You know exactly what they're gonna do, what they're gonna say, what they're gonna wear, and everything else. If I make it as an actor and hang out in L.A., you won't catch me going to all those lame Hollywood parties or premieres. You go to a premiere or opening and you see all the same stars, over and over and over. It's the same boring circle, and I hate going to their parties because it's all about who looks the best, who knows the most people, who has the most influence, who has this or who has that.

Well, fuck that. I might as well hang out with a bunch of politicians. Or athletes. And you know that's the last thing I'm ever going to do.

Ten

Hypnotize the Enemy

FRANK **B**RICKOWSKI MADE ONE HELL OF A MIS-
TAKE, **AND I MADE HIM PAY.** It was the second quarter of game 1 of the 1995–96 NBA Finals, and
Brickowski walked onto the floor of the United Center thinking
he could get inside my head.

George Karl, the coach of the Seattle Supersonics, is a cool
guy who I get along with great, and a crazy bastard too. But
George should have known better than to send Brickowski into
the game with the sole purpose of trying to take me out of
mine.

It can't be done. **NO ONE CAN TAKE ME OUT OF
MY GAME EXCEPT ME.** But Brickowski tried, right there
in front of everyone, and I taught him and everyone else on the
Sonics a painful lesson.

The first thing Brickowski did when he came into the game
was walk straight up to me and say, "Bet you can't wait until the
game's over so somebody can fuck you right in the ass."

I looked him in the eye and answered him slowly, calmly:
"Would you like to be the one?"

I have nothing against Brickowski. He's not a bad guy at all.
But he was out of his league. I haven't won three championships, five rebounding titles, and two defensive player of the
year awards because I'm physically superior to everyone else.

The only reason I've been able to accomplish anything is because my mental makeup is so strong. Whether I'm fighting Charles Barkley for a rebound or waging war with David Stern, THE KEY TO THE STRUGGLE IS WINNING THE BATTLE OF THE BRAINS.

Am I the smartest guy in the world? Hell, no. In terms of being book-smart or educated, I'm pretty much of a washout. I don't read much, and I don't know shit about Ernest Hemingway, except that his granddaughter, Mariel, did some great topless scenes in *Star 80*. I could probably tell you more about George Jefferson than I could Thomas Jefferson. I've learned a lot of things in my life, but I've forgotten about two thirds of them.

But I do think I'm street-smart. I know I have good instincts. I'm pretty thoughtful about most things, and I trip on various ideas because I'm willing to step outside the mental boundaries that most people set up and check things out from a different lookout point. Still, my ability to mess with the Frank Brickowskis of the world, or the Shaquille O'Neals, has more to do with mental toughness and discipline than it does intelligence.

Athletes have different ways of psyching themselves up to compete. What I do is I harness all of the pain that I've gone through in my life and turn the game into a survival test. I also concentrate on a twisted level that allows me to step outside the hectic happenings of the game and feel the energy. One reason I'm a great rebounder is that I can exist in a zone where I'm at one with the ball, and I have a cosmic sense of where it's going.

Probably the most important part of my mental game is the way I do battle with the person in my path. **IN BASKETBALL AND IN LIFE, I HYPNOTIZE THE ENEMY.** People, especially athletes, get so caught up in the concept of intimidation that they miss the big picture. What I do is beyond intimidation; I'm too smart to get caught up in that bullshit. Instead I hypnotize people. Many of them don't even know it's happening. I make them think about things other than the task at hand, like what I'm thinking about or why I'm acting the way I do. Then, when I'm physically beating them, they're thrown off enough that they don't know how to react properly or calmly. That's when I've won.

I do this every time I play, but the Brickowski incident was classic. Actually, the whole series was. The Sonics were underdogs who hadn't been to the finals before, while many of us—myself, Michael Jordan, Scottie Pippen, Phil Jackson, John Salley, and James Edwards—had won multiple championships in the past. We had set an NBA record with seventy-two victories, and it's easy to see why the Sonics might have been intimidated, especially with the series starting on our home floor. There are different ways to deal with that feeling. One is talk a lot of shit and act like you belong and hope no one calls your bluff. Another strategy is to try to create tension within the other team, and a good way to do that is to pick the craziest, most emotional guy on the court—the one who recently had been suspended for head-butting a ref—and try to get him to snap.

So George Karl sent Brickowski in to go after me. George must have figured that Brickowski isn't that valuable of a player, so if the guy could pick a fight and get us both kicked out, it would be a great trade-off for the Sonics. First Frank tried to rattle me with words, but there was no way that was gonna work. Then he tried to get physical with me, and all I did was push back. It was so obvious what was going on that I would've had to have been a total fool to fall for it. I've been known to do volatile things during a game, but *IT'S NOT LIKE I'M SOME OUT-OF-CONTROL MANIAC CAPABLE OF SNAPPING AT ANY TIME.* There's a method to my madness, and I only SNAP ON MY OWN TERMS.

PIGGYBACK JACK

Everyone thinks Jack Haley, my former teammate with the Bulls and Spurs, is my best friend and guardian angel. Jack and I have had a lot of fun hanging out together, but I believe the whole myth about him taking care of me exists because he created it.

Jack was the only guy on the Spurs I could deal with, and after I got traded to Chicago, the Bulls signed him basically as a mascot. People think I asked the Bulls to sign him, but there's no way I would do that. I guess the Bulls signed Jack because they thought he could keep an eye on me. What a joke. Jack's a good guy, and we go out and party sometimes and have a blast together. But Jack benefits greatly from his association with me. He's an opportunist that way, and that's why he could be called Piggyback Jack.

Toward the end of the season, all of us on the Bulls got together to divvy up playoff shares. Usually, what happens is that guys who have been with the team part of the season will get like a three fourths share or half a share or something like that. Well,

Walk On The Wild Side

Jack was on the injured list all season, until the very end, when he got activated. He ended up playing seven minutes of one game—he scored five points, got two rebounds and made a turnover. He wasn't exactly a major contributor, but the guy got an incredible amount of publicity, and that wasn't lost on the rest of the players. Jack is always the guy running out to high-five someone or standing up and whooping it up on the bench after a nice play—in other words, it seemed like he was always looking for airtime. So when his name came up in that meeting to decide playoff shares, people pretty much wanted to give him nothing, because they figured he'd already gotten way more than he deserved. A few people looked over to see if I'd stick up for him, and I said, "We've got to give him something." So the guy got $10,000 and a ring, basically for standing up and waving his hands.

I don't see how Piggyback Jack can argue with that.

If Brickowski had understood my history, he wouldn't even have bothered trying to provoke me. When you're living in the projects and you've got no money, you either sink or swim. If you swim, it's because you develop an incredible amount of mental discipline. How else would I have been able to deal with the racists who harassed me when I played for Southeastern Oklahoma State if I wasn't mentally strong?

The great thing about the Brickowski incident is that when he finally snapped, I wasn't even the guy pushing him over the edge. He had picked up a couple of quick fouls for pushing me around, and then the ref gave him a technical for a flagrant foul after he pushed me out of bounds by our bench. The crowd was on him in a big way, and when the crowd is on a guy, Jack Haley, in his sharp suit, will be on him even worse. Good old Piggyback Jack had risen from his seat on our bench to yell at Frank, telling him to stop messing with me, and Frank just lost it. He yelled back at Jack, **"WHAT ARE YOU, HIS FUCKING BABY-SITTER?"** Good line, bad move. Brickowski got a second technical and an automatic ejection. When a guy who doesn't even play can get you kicked out of an NBA Finals game, that's pretty pathetic. But hey, **GIVE JACK SOME CREDIT. THAT'S DEFINITELY THE MOST VALUABLE THING HE DID FOR US ALL SEASON.**

Brickowski didn't learn, and I messed with him the next two games as well. He got kicked out of game 3 for going after me. It was too easy, and for a while, their whole team was sort of mesmerized by my aura. Seattle's star forward, Shawn Kemp, even got caught in my web. But it didn't affect him that badly, because he went out and played his ass off. Kemp is a guy who wants to be respected and he should be. He was young as hell when he came into the league and didn't know what it took to be a champion. But he figured it out, worked hard, and now he's a leader. I respect him for that—even if I did have him a little mind-fucked during the finals.

Knowing how and when to respond to a challenge isn't just something that applies to a basketball game. People taunt and test each other every day, and everyone has to exercise self-control on a regular basis. I'm the last guy in the world to get on people for losing their cool, but I will say this: **NEVER SNAP ON SOMEONE ELSE'S TERMS**. If you know in your heart that you're losing it for a good reason, even if that reason is to blow off steam and keep yourself from going insane, and you're willing to accept the consequences, then knock yourself out. But if someone else is pushing you into doing something that's not in your best interests, don't let them get away with it. The best way to make sure they don't is to stay in control.

Most people think I'm an out-of-control madman who's always one step away from blowing his head off. I have no problem with this image, but the truth is there's almost always a method to my madness. Take the two incidents that got me in trouble during the 1996–97 season: my swearing episode on live TV after I was kicked out of a game in Toronto, and the kick to the leg I delivered to a cameraman in Minnesota. I got suspended for both incidents and lost well over $1 million in the process, but I knew what I was doing, and I had my reasons. Everything can be traced back to the frustration that results from trying to survive in a league whose power brokers want you to eat shit and die.

The way I see it, David Stern thinks that because he's the NBA commissioner with a big, fat contract, he can do whatever he wants. He thinks. It's his league. I'm no angel, but he does seem to single me out. It's so obvious to me he wants people like Shaquille O'Neal and Grant Hill to succeed because they smile and behave and fall into line with the goody-two-shoes image the league is trying to project. I think the league has

MAKING DAVID STERN'S LIFE DIFFICULT

a problem with me because I insist on not kissing ass and being my own person, and because I'm more popular than ever. Every time I succeed, it proves that there's plenty of room in the NBA, and in life, for a nonconformist who does things his own way.

I would like to party with Stern one night and see if he has a soul. Just before our '96–97 home opener against the Philadelphia 76ers, Stern was there to present us with our championship rings. When I got mine he reached out to shake my hand, and I left him hanging. I was making a statement about the way I feel. He and other members of the establishment treat me like a wayward stepchild. And it's not just Stern. The way I see it, there is an entire propaganda machine waging war against me. Take, for example, the #1 midget on television. BOB COSTAS OF NBC CAN DO ME WITH HIS MICROPHONE. I don't know what his story is. I think **HE'S GOT SHORT-MAN'S COMPLEX.** He kisses more ass than the average politician. ***Bob Costas can lick my balls, and the great thing is, he can do it standing up.***

The sad thing is, Stern, Costas, and company are probably going to win, because I just don't have the energy to fight them night in and night out. I've got enough going in my life outside of basketball that I can walk away from the game, if not now then soon. I just don't need the headaches anymore. Nobody can treat me any worse than I've been treated at some times in my life, but after a while you just get worn down. I just get tired of the same routine, over and over and over, and the bullshit and the politics that go along with it. You can't fight the system forever, and the young players who come into the league nowadays are making it worse. They don't know what winning is all about, and they're just into their own thing.

The refs are a constant pain in the ass. There used to be a lot of great officials that stood on their own two feet, guys like Jake O'Don- nell and Earl Strom. But now most of the refs I respect are gone, and there's a new crop of suck-asses. I know a lot of them aren't bad people, and I respect how tough their job is. You might think I sound para- noid, but **I THINK THE REFS DEFI- NITELY TREAT ME MORE HARSHLY THAN OTHER PLAYERS** and I often wonder if the powers that be have let it be known that's what's supposed to happen. I don't have any hard proof, but I bet it's true. Now the league is talking about having women refs, which is very interesting to me. What I'm wondering is, who's gonna be the first brother to fuck one of them? You know

REFS GET ME AGAIN

156

the players will get a pool going and someone will do it just to be the guy who did.

When I head-butted the ref late in the '95–96 season, it wasn't so much that I was pissed off about the call. It just struck me as something that would feel good at the time and that needed to be done. It felt good that I could just go out there and be myself. I was making a statement that I was free and independent and not like everybody else.

In December of '96 I lashed back at the refs again. We were playing a game in Toronto, and I protested a foul call by throwing my hands up over my head in exasperation. **If Michael Jordan or Shaquille O'Neal or pretty much anyone else had done this, I BET NOTHING WOULD HAVE HAPPENED.** But I got a technical and was kicked out of the game. It was typical, and after the game ended I was still steamed. I didn't snap or anything—again, I knew exactly what I was doing—but in very calm and deliberate tones, in a postgame TV interview, I told the world exactly what I felt about the system. I used a lot of profanity; hell, I must have said the F-word about twenty-five times.

There were only a couple of problems. First, unbeknownst to me, the interview was broadcast on live TV back to Chicago by SportsChannel, which has a show called *Live in the Locker Room*. And secondly, not only did SportsChannel stay with the interview long after I said the first "fuck," their reporter asked a follow-up question. At the end of the interview, I was blowing off steam for years of feeling like I was the NBA's fall guy and said, **"BASICALLY, *David Stern can fuck off.*"** You think he didn't go apeshit over that? The Bulls ended up suspending me for two games for excessive profanity, and I'd put my money that the league was behind it. Although I can't say this for a fact, it wouldn't surprise me in the least if someone called up our general manager, Jerry Krause, and said, "If you don't suspend him right now, I will."

I apologized publicly for the incident, but I didn't view it as a major mistake on my part. Everyone talks about how little kids had to hear me using all that profanity, but I don't worry about kids. **KIDS ARE GOING TO COME TO THEIR OWN JUDGMENT,** regardless of what they're told is right and wrong. They'll say, "Well, you know, that guy's defending his own rights, and that's what I should do. He doesn't do anything too weird or too corrupt that's hurting anybody, so it's cool."

I'M THE LAST PERSON WHO WANTS TO BE A ROLE MODEL, but I do know that a lot of kids, particularly the misfits of society, look up to me because they know I won't kiss anyone's ass. I used the F-word to show everyone exactly how upset I am by the situation. I get so sick and tired of people telling me, "Be calm, Dennis, everything will work itself out." In my case, it will never be worked out, because the league is always going to try to fuck me over, and I'll never be the goody-goody they want me to be.

Then, **ON JANUARY 15, I MUST HAVE GIVEN DAVID**

STERN THE **BIGGEST WOODY** HE'S EVER HAD. We were playing a game in Minnesota and I was going for a rebound under the basket when this in-house cameraman for the Timberwolves got in my way. The guy was right there underneath the basket, and I stepped on him and turned my ankle. I was pissed; anyone would be. A fluke injury like that can end a career. So I kicked his camera and my foot continued up to his thigh. It was probably a little bit of an overreaction, but I was caught up in the heat of the moment, and to me it was just another sign of the way the league cares more about its image than its players—especially a player like me who doesn't fall into line.

Anyway, this guy claims I kicked him in the groin. He was pissed as hell, but then it looked to me like a cash register clicked in his head and he went down on the ground, writhing in pain. You would've thought the **GUY GOT KNOCKED OUT** by Mike Tyson. It was pathetic. He was there for about eight minutes and then he got carried out on a stretcher. What an embarrassment. I've been hurt many times in my life, and I always leave under my own power as a point of pride. But here's this guy who seemed to be milking the moment for all it was worth, playing the part of the victim to a T. When he first went down, I said to him, "Sorry I kicked you, bro." He looked up and whined, "Get away from me!" I shrugged and got back to the game.

Obviously, the guy was planning to sue my ass. Knowing this

crazy country, he probably would have claimed I gave him whiplash and tennis elbow, too. Shortly after the incident he was asking for several hundred thousand dollars and I ended up settling with him for $200,000. Two hundred thousand dollars! In other words, **FIVE KICKS IN THE PANTS and YOU CAN BECOME A MILLIONAIRE.** I know I broke my own rule when I lost my cool, but how much do you have to pay for your mistakes? In my case, the punishment definitely did not fit the crime.

Let's review: A few years ago, Charles Barkley spit at a fan who was heckling him from a courtside seat and missed. He hit a young girl in the face instead. Did the league suspend him? Nay.

A couple of years after that, Houston's Vernon Maxwell charged into the stands during a game in Portland and punched a heckler. He was suspended ten games.

I got an eleven-game suspension, and that wasn't all. The league ordered me to go to counseling, and David Stern said I'd have to convince him and the counselor that I was ready to return to the court before he'd let me back in the league. **IT WAS A JOKE,** and everyone around the league knew it.

This all went down around the time Michael Jordan said that all of my outside interests were taking my attention away from basketball and that I needed to regain my focus. Was I pissed off at him for saying that? Hell, no. First of all, I had already said the same thing. Secondly, consider the source. **IS THERE ANY-**

ONE IN THE WORLD WITH MORE OUTSIDE INTER- ESTS THAN MICHAEL JORDAN? What about HIS movie, *Space Jam*, or his new cologne, or his millions of endorsements? He's a true expert on that subject.

See, Michael and I are both strong enough that we can be critical of one another in the media and shrug it off. The same thing goes for Scottie Pippen. I've never had a legitimate conversation with either Michael or Scottie, but we respect each other's auras and give each other space. After my suspension in Toronto, Scottie said that it's hard enough for my teammates to keep me in line, let alone the refs. I didn't love what he said, but it didn't bother me. Scottie's not a person who could bother me if he tried. Besides, he was mistaken.

I'M JUST A FLAMBOYANT, FREE-SPIRIT, JIMI HENDRIX/JIM MORRISON WILD MAN WRAPPED INTO ONE—

but I'm not uncontrollable. If I was uncontrollable, I'd be pulling my pants down during games and all sorts of crazy shit.

Just like with Michael, Scottie and I respect each other to the point where we can say negative things or positive things and still be on the same wavelength. I have no problems with Scottie voicing his opinion. For some reason, he's always been caught in the middle—he's not quite Michael, but he's still a strong presence—and he doesn't really seem comfortable. He should be, though. He's one of the best players this league's ever had. He's so versatile, he might be the best all-around player in the league. Anyway, Scottie and Michael were on the right track. I managed to put myself back in the focused mode, because I didn't want to let my teammates down.

People can take verbal shots at me all they want, on or off the court. After all I've been through in my life, I know someone else's words are never going to faze me, so I have fun with the whole process. When I do talk trash, I'm not like most players who get right up in your face and do it with flair. Michael Jordan and Gary Payton were going back and forth like that during the finals, but that's not my style. Instead, I come up with something either really nasty or very weird and I say it real low so only the guy I'm talking to can hear it and no one else. Like, if I'm playing David Benoit of the New Jersey Nets, I might make a comment about benwa balls. I'll say it so quietly that he won't know whether to laugh or get pissed, and no one else can get involved. That way, we just have our own private thing going on.

He knows I'm not doing it for show or because I'm scared of him deep inside or as an intimidation device. ***I'm just giving him a little something to think about.***

In February of 1996, right after Magic Johnson came out of retirement to rejoin the Lakers, we played them in L.A. It was Magic's second game back, and I respect him as much as anyone who has ever played, but that didn't stop me from talking to him. I said, "What are you finally playing for? You know what this means. It means your ass will get kicked even worse than before. I'm gonna double-kick your ass now." He just said, "Well, bring it on," and then we both played our asses off. I had 23 rebounds and we won by 15, and Magic and I hugged after the game. All I did was treat him like a competitor, and that's all he can ask for. If there's anyone who knows about mental toughness, it's him, so we were just showing each other respect.

I can't say I have the SAME RESPECT for SHAQUILLE O'NEAL, who fell into my mental trap during the '95–96 playoffs. We beat the Orlando Magic in the Eastern Conference Finals four games to none, and it looked like Shaq was worrying about every little thing I did. Like a lot of players, I find him easy to mess with, and he's even easier in some ways because HE TAKES HIMSELF SO DAMN SERIOUSLY.

Right now **I VIEW SHAQ AS A WHOLE LOT OF HYPE.** In my opinion, he has to stop getting caught up in all the bullshit and prove himself as a player who has the mental toughness to take his team to the top, and even though he's now on the Lakers, who are pretty good, I'm not sure if that will happen. He doesn't have my respect yet, and a lot of guys have told me they respect me more than Shaq. I know he can dunk the ball and all that, but I think he's all flash. To me, he's a wanna-be, but the league still loves to promote him, and he's a very rich wanna-be.

I really wasn't saying shit to Shaq on the court, but I was talking about him to reporters after the games, picking at his weaknesses, and I know it was getting to him from his responses. I used the same line Michael Jordan ended up using on me the next season: "The guy has rap albums and a movie career and every endorsement in the world. How badly can he want to win?" I laughed when Michael said that stuff about me, because I've won three championships. But you could tell Shaq was listening to what I was saying because he'd talk right back at me through the media. He tried to come after me and stab me in certain areas, and I was like, "Go ahead." I loved every bit of it—it meant he was involving himself in my mental game instead of starting one on his own.

One night last summer in L.A., I walked into a club called Peanuts on Santa Monica Boulevard and sat down in a booth. About an hour later Shaq walked in and sat down in the booth next to me. I got up and went to a different booth. A few minutes later, he came up to me and said, "What's up?" I said, "Oh, now you want to talk to me. You didn't want to speak to me during the playoffs, but all of a sudden you want to be my buddy now." I was mostly just busting his balls, but I do think *HE CAN BE A BIT OF A PHONY.* Now he's in L.A., which is the perfect place for him.

Maybe Shaq took it personally, because the first time we played them in the '96–97 season, he went after me on the court. He shoved me, and I got up in his face, and Michael and Scottie tackled me to keep me from getting kicked out. But **I WASN'T GOING TO BACK DOWN TO HIM OR ANYONE ELSE.** Sure, Shaq is a hell of a lot bigger than me, and he intimidates a lot of people with his size and strength. My attitude is, I've survived a lot worse than some 300-pound dude pushing me around the paint. Shit like that doesn't even faze me, and that freaks some people out. Maybe it freaked Shaq out. Maybe he wanted to take a swing at me. What the hell was I supposed to do, be afraid? You can't be. You just play.

`Pain doesn't scare me.` I know pain well, and I use it to my advantage every day. If you've ever gotten tattooed, you know what pain is. I'd say that if someone gets tattooed all over his body, he has a high tolerance for pain. I always push myself to the point of pain in my workouts, because it makes me tougher mentally. I know that no one can bring me more pain than I bring to myself, except for my daughter, and that's a powerful feeling to carry with me into battle.

I try to inflict pain on myself, mentally and physically, on a daily basis, and then I can go out there and challenge everybody else. No one can hurt me then.

Then there's Charles Barkley, another guy who knows how to play the mental game. When he and I go up against each other, we say all kinds of funny shit back and forth, just to keep it interesting. He'll say, "Who the fuck do you think you are?" and I'll just laugh. With a guy like him I mostly just want to play, because talking to him is a no-win situation—you're not gonna mess with him, because he's too sharp. Then again, trying to mess with me is a no-win situation, because I've seen it all, heard it all, and done it all.

There are a lot of things I admire about Charles. He forms an opinion and takes a stand, and he's done it for so long that no one's gonna do shit to try to stop him, the way the NBA tries to keep the wraps on me. But sometimes I think Charles gets caught up in a lot of stuff that he doesn't necessarily believe in. He projects this crazy image, but we went out one night in Phoenix—the night before I played drunk against the Suns—and I couldn't believe how tame he was. ***He's not nearly AS WILD as I thought he would be.*** As I said before, I don't judge people on how much they drink. But I expected Charles to be a little more adventurous, because that's how he projects himself in public. Then again, it might have been a bad night. All in all, Charles Barkley is one of the coolest dudes around, and the NBA would be much better off if there were more people like him.

At the start of the '96–97 season Charles got ahead of me in

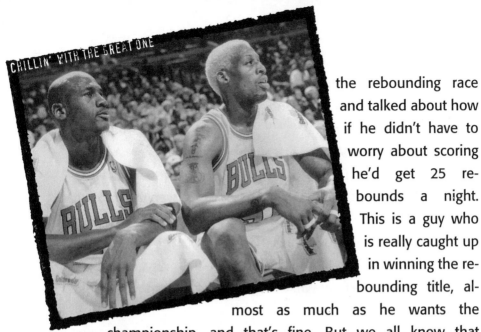

the rebounding race and talked about how if he didn't have to worry about scoring he'd get 25 rebounds a night. This is a guy who is really caught up in winning the rebounding title, almost as much as he wants the championship, and that's fine. But we all know that **WINNING THE CHAMPIONSHIP IS ALL THAT MATTERS, AND CHARLES STILL HASN'T DONE THAT.** Early in the season, I issued a public challenge to Charles: whichever one of us didn't win the rebounding title would have to wear a dress. He said no way, which didn't surprise me. It's too bad, because it would have been pretty comical.

It helps when you have Michael Jordan on your team, because he's not only the best there is at playing the mind game, he's obsessed with it. Oh, and one other thing: **HE'S THE BEST BASKETBALL PLAYER OF ALL TIME,** and I don't make that statement lightly, not with the way I've studied the great players of the past.

As I've said, Michael and I don't really talk, but there's a common respect. I'm pretty sure he likes having me around because it means there's more than one circus in town. That takes some of the pressure off of him, and he's too strong to feel threatened. He has his own tribe, and it's all over the world, so he's not threatened by anything.

Some people say Michael is a control freak, but I can sniff out people like that from a mile away, and he doesn't seem like one to me. He's more of a perfectionist who wants everything to run smoothly, that's all. He doesn't tell me what to do. Even after I got suspended for head-butting that ref late in the '95–96 season, all he wanted to know from me was my mindset. It was more like, "I don't know what you're thinking, but what would make you do that?"

At the start of the '96–97 season, some quotes critical of me that were attributed to Michael came out in a book called *In the Year of the Bull*. It was written by Rick Telander of the *Chicago Sun Times*, a writer who has been out with me a few times and likes to get a little wild himself. Rick is cool, but I have a hard time imagining that Michael called me an asshole. What Michael supposedly told Rick was this: "He views himself as being special, unique, an entertainer. I don't buy everything, and he knows it. You can tell by the way he plays he's an asshole. Like getting kicked out of games. You see him at the half or in the third quarter with five, four, three rebounds, you can believe he's gonna go off. Because he doesn't feel he has the spotlight." He also says that the team has to fight me to get rebounds and that my offensive rebounding comes from me aborting the offense.

Two reactions: First, if Michael really was that down on me

last year, I would've heard about it. Michael sat next to George Triantafillo, one of my bodyguards, on the flight home from Seattle during the Finals and talked to him about all kinds of shit, straight-out, for four hours. He told George that if he had a choice between me and Charles Barkley, who's a close personal friend of his, he'd take me on his team. **HE SAID A LOT OF THINGS ABOUT ME, AND THE WORD ASSHOLE WAS NEVER USED.**

My second reaction is, even if he did say that stuff, I don't give a shit. Michael and I both want to win; we don't have to be lovers or anything. Besides, I take bad criticism better than I take good criticism. Bad criticism gives you the inspiration to fight. Even if you're on top of your game or on top of the world, you still have something to give you motivation. It keeps you on the spot so that you can just keep going and proving yourself time and time again. All I know is that Telander's book has my picture on the back cover, all dressed up in drag, and I'm signing MY book. So I might be an asshole, but I'm an asshole who people want to read about, I guess.

Eleven

Be a Two-Way Player

*S*ince there's one question everyone wants to know, I'll just come right out and answer it.

YES, I'M GAY.

Feel better? Well, there's a second answer.

I'M STRAIGHT.

Confused? Me, too. It must be nice for people who are so sure about their orientation. In my case it's more complex. It's not easy for me to put a tag on my sexuality. I guess if I had to give one answer, I'd say that I'm bisexual, which is hardly a shocking statement. I think deep inside we're all bisexual, whether people are willing to admit it or not. And when I say bisexual, I don't just mean that I'm attracted to members of both sexes. I mean that **I'M IN TOUCH with BOTH MY MASCULINE and FEMININE SIDES.**

I am both strong and sensitive, macho and bitchy, aggressive and submissive. I show my feminine side to the public at times, partly to make a statement, and partly because it helps me to feel whole. But it is always with me, and if I had to go through a day without it I'd be a lost soul. The way I look at it is, Why deny yourself the whole enchilada? **BE A TWO-WAY PLAYER,** and you'll be better balanced, more comfortable, and more interesting than someone who thinks he can only go one direction.

When I had my wedding ceremony in Manhattan in the summer of '96, everyone saw it as a cheap publicity stunt. But I truly was marrying my fans. So many **people think I'm strange for being so in touch with my feminine side,** but I don't see anything unusual about it at all. What seems really weird to me is all the men who suppress and ignore that part of their personality because they've bought into the myth that men can't show any weaknesses. They deny their sensitivity. They won't let anyone see them cry, like that's some sort of embarrassing act. *I THINK CRYING IS BEAUTIFUL.* It's a very healthy process. You

SHINING ON MY WEDDING DAY

have to flush out your system, and that's why every month or so I have a good, long cry. One night in L.A. a couple of years ago I was drunk as hell and ended up breaking down in Cousin Al's arms and sobbing like a baby for forty-five minutes. It would be hard for most men in our culture to admit something like that, because they're taught to put up a rugged front. They're afraid to say, "I love you," or to hug another man, even if it's their father, their brother, or their son. A lot of men are homophobic as hell, even though every single one of them would love to see two women lick each other all over. Anyone who says he wouldn't want to see that is either impotent or a liar. Most men get a hard-on just thinking about it.

It's hard for men especially to deal with my cross-dressing and my effeminate tendencies, but that's not my problem. Guys, **HERE'S A SECRET:** Chicks absolutely love it. Believe me, I know. ***When women see a man comfortable with both sides of his sexuality, they know he'll be creative and adventurous in bed, and it turns them on.***

Most men react to the stuff I do by making jokes about it. How many times have you turned on *The Tonight Show* or Letterman and heard a one-liner about my cross-dressing or gay tendencies? It has gotten ridiculous the way people have just been overwhelmed by some of the stuff I've done. Everyone jokes about it, but very few people come out and say, "You know, you're very in touch with your inner being, and I admire you for being so upfront about that." But you know what? People, especially other famous people, say that to ME all the time. Still, in the public realm, it has to be a joke. I can take a joke as well as the next guy, but it's the SAME JOKE, over and over. It's like saying the word "underwear" and getting laughs the fiftieth time. At some point it's just not that funny anymore.

People have to joke about it because the subject makes them uncomfortable. **A LOT OF PEOPLE ARE SCARED OF ME, BECAUSE I BRING OUT FEELINGS AND IDEAS THAT THEY'D PREFER TO KEEP HIDDEN.** Seeing me in drag or hanging out with gay men forces a lot of people to deal with an area they're afraid to confront. This is especially true because of the way male athletes are expected to behave. We are supposed to be these macho supermen who stand for the American way. Men want their sons to grow up to be Michael Jordan or Troy Aikman. But if their boys grow up to be like Dennis Rodman . . . well, that's scary to most people, because they're afraid of the unknown. It's easier to make a joke out of it and turn it into a cliché, so that's what they do.

But **THE TRUTH IS,** guys are feminine. That's not the way they're portrayed, and some of them don't allow that side of themselves to surface, but it's true. Most men are scared of their feminine side, and that's why they react so strongly to gays or people like me who support gay rights. I GET CALLED A FAG EVERY SINGLE DAY, as if I'm supposed to be ashamed of it. It's because I'm an athlete and sports are the testosterone capital of society, even though in reality male athletes are hugging and grabbing each

"DARE TO BE DIFFERENT"

other and patting each other on the ass all the time. So call me a fag—I enjoy it, because it means I've gotten people to think about the issue. **Every time I hear that word, I know I'm on the right track.** There are plenty of in-the-closet athletes, and their sexual preference has nothing to do with their courage or heart or competitiveness. The funny thing is, all athletes go out there believing they're indestructible, that they have these strong, superhuman bodies that can't be harmed. But when a guy gets injured, all of a sudden he's the most sensitive, emotional man in the world. These big, tough athletes will be down on the ground moaning in pain and looking scared as kittens without their mamas because their livelihoods are on the line. I think it's cool when people are forced to reveal their vulnerabilities, because then they seem more real. But most people would rather just say, "He's a fag," and perpetuate the myth, because it's easier.

When people wonder whether I'm gay, what most of them really want to know is, ***HAVE I HAD SEX WITH A MAN?*** If I had, I would not be embarrassed in the least. But the answer is no. **I'VE KISSED MEN,** and I've fantasized about being with a man many times. But have I ever given a blow job, or received one from a man, or had anal sex with a dude? **NOT YET.**

The main reason that I haven't done any of this—so far—is that I've been so preoccupied with the interesting and attractive women in my life. Sex with women is very exciting to me, partly because I don't have enough sex to be bored by it. Most people, when they get really bored with the opposite sex, their natural reaction is to see what the same sex can do for them. If I was bored with women, my asshole would be very fucking large right now.

I'm not sure whether I'll be with a man in the future, but it's something I've definitely been thinking about for a while. `IF I EVER DO DECIDE TO HAVE SEX WITH A MAN, I'LL FIND A GUY JUST LIKE ME AND LOVE THE SHIT OUT OF HIM.` It'll be like two bulls going at it, bro, I'll tell you that.

`Would I care about dick size?` **HELL, YEAH, I WOULD.** Most girls want a guy with a big penis, that's plain and simple, so why should a man be any different?

If you're gonna go down that road, you have no choice but to go big. You go for the mountaintop, the big sword, Daddy Long Dong. I say, "Bring it on." Guys are always talking about dick size, but they'd never admit they're interested in each other's schlongs. Yet everyone in the locker room looks at each other's rods, just like any time you're in a shower with a bunch of guys, you check each other out. You may not be sexually aroused, but you're curious. That's just common sense.

Anal sex doesn't gross me out, because I've done it to women and they've seemed to like it. I know it's been good for me. As long as you're practicing safe sex and your partner likes it and you know what sex is all about, it's perfectly OK. And anal sex is not always some major event that's planned. If I slip, I slip. Oh well.

As for the oral sex part, what's so gross about that? I ask guys all the time, "If you were kicking back on the beach with your eyes closed and someone came up and gave you the best blow job ever, would it really matter if it was a guy or girl? Or an animal, for that matter?" They always say it would matter, and when I ask them why, they say, "It just would." I say that's bullshit. It wouldn't matter at all. ***Good head is good head.***

A friend of mine just had his dick sucked by a transvestite for five weeks straight and then found out it was a guy. Five goddamn weeks, and he didn't know. And he said, "Ah, fuck," and he thought it was disgusting. I told him, "but you must have thought it was great because you kept doing it."

I put it like this: **YOU PUT A BLINDFOLD OVER TWO MEN WITH SOFT LIPS, AND I GUARANTEE THEY COULDN'T TELL WHETHER THEY WERE KISSING A GUY OR A GIRL.** I know, because I've kissed guys with soft lips before. I'm not afraid to admit that. Maybe that means that I'm still searching to uncover secrets about my own sexuality. I'm not claiming to know all the answers. But if I'm with a guy, especially if we're just playing around, why is that even an issue? It's an exploration process I have to go through. I don't see why people on the outside even care.

People are always trying to figure out why I'm into cross-dressing and flaunting my femininity. Is it because I grew up in a female-dominated household, with my mother and two sisters? Well, my sisters

did use to dress me up in women's clothes, so that could be part of it. Or is it because I hung out with Madonna and picked up some of her tricks? Well, **I LOVE WHAT MADONNA HAS DONE FOR THE GAY COMMUNITY,** but I felt this way before I went out with her. Some people wonder if it's because I was sexually abused as a child. Well . . .

This is very tough for me to talk about, because I think I've blocked some incidents from my past out of my memory. But *I KEEP HAVING THIS VISION THAT I'VE HAD SEX WITH A MAN BEFORE, BACK WHEN I WAS A KID, AND LATELY THE VISION HAS SEEMED MORE AND MORE VIVID.* I'm into visualization, anyway, and I've been trying to dig deeper and deeper into my memory bank to figure out what might have happened. **IN THE VISION I'm being violated by someone I know, but I can't see his face.** I'm not in control of what's happening, and I want him to stop, but I'm scared, so I just let it happen.

I'm a little hesitant to say this definitely happened, because I tend to have a very creative imagination. But my gut feeling is that it did. If I can dredge up this memory, it's going to be pretty freaky. I mean, what if I see the man's face in one of my visions? Will I try to kill the guy? Will I track him down and just try to talk to him? I know what he did was bad, but should I also thank him for making me more in tune with an issue I might have ignored otherwise?

There are no cut-and-dried answers. It's like that line from

"Lola," that old song by the Kinks about the guy who gets picked up by a transvestite: "Girls will be boys and boys will be girls.," Take my friend Mimi, who used to be named Michael. When I met her she was a man, but I didn't know at first, because she's one of the most striking, voluptuous blondes I have ever seen. When Mimi first saw me, she said, "I want to meet that guy because I would like to fuck him. **I want him to be my boy for a day.**" She came right up and said this so I could hear her. I said, "Thank you." It didn't faze me. I hear stuff like that all the time. A LOT OF MEN WANT TO FUCK ME. A LOT OF WOMEN WANT TO FUCK ME. A LOT OF MEN THAT TRY TO BE WOMEN WANT TO FUCK ME. I'M USED TO IT.

I HAD BEEN WITH MIMI A COUPLE OF TIMES BEFORE I REALIZED THAT SHE WAS A MAN. It turns out she was on the road to becoming a woman. She took hormones and had a couple of surgeries, and we've stayed close throughout the process. It was intriguing in the beginning. We've kissed before, and I'm not ashamed to admit she turns me on. To be around her, as beautiful as she is, I'd have no problem going further with her. It wouldn't freak me out that she's been surgically altered. To me **SEX IS A VIBE,** anyway, **not some clinical act.**

I think Mimi's cool as shit. Just because she used to be a man and now she's a woman, it doesn't mean that she's not the same person inside. We have a lot in common, because a lot of people look at her like she's a freak and whisper about her as she walks by. Both of us were tired of living as someone we didn't want to be.

The funny thing is there's no way in hell I'd ever want to be a woman. Then I'd have to deal with assholes like me and every other guy out there trying to screw every woman in sight. **When you put yourself in a woman's shoes and look at what she has to put up with, it's not a pretty picture.** Remember what I said about men: We want to fuck the woman so badly, but as soon as we spread our seed, we want to be left alone. The woman wants to cuddle and be held and fulfill her emotional needs, and the man is thinking about making a sandwich or changing the channel or screwing her best friend—or he's already asleep. It's easier being a man, because on some levels we're just not that deep. We might have principles and philosophies and convictions, but

COULD YOU TELL THE DIFFERENCE? . . . WITH MIMI

we'll sell them all down the river if it helps us get our rocks off. It means so much to us to have a hot-looking woman giving us some action, making us feel like a stud, that it blinds us to common sense. Then, when the conquest is over, we want something new. I know this sounds like a convenient excuse, but men know it's true. Some of us are able to fight against our nature and treat women responsibly, but it takes work.

Women get fucked over a lot by men, but they're partly to blame for letting it happen. As an athlete, I see women who just set themselves up to be trampled on and don't even have a shred of dignity. One night I was partying at Crobar and sort of hanging out with this one woman. But she didn't like the fact that other women were coming onto me and rubbing my ass. So she threw a big tantrum, announced that she was leaving and stormed off. Then she came back. A few minutes later, she made the same speech and left again. She did this five times in a forty-five-minute span. That's what's known as lack of leverage.

IF WOMEN REALLY WANTED TO RULE THE WORLD, THEY COULD DO IT, because they have the power. *THEY'RE THE ONES WHO CONTROL THE PUSSY, AND MOST MEN WILL SELL THEIR SOULS JUST TO GET SOME.* And they're the ones who can reproduce, which is truly the most potent power known to humanity. Guys should be treating women better, but the sad fact is we don't. So, if they really want to be treated better, the women should realize the extent of their powers and start using that leverage to get more of what they want. And if the men don't like it, they can probably get by without us.

Now I'm starting to sound like a lesbian, which isn't a coincidence. I definitely have some lesbian tendencies. When I dress up, it makes me feel soft and sexy, and the thought of touching another tender body is a major turn-on. When it comes to sexuality, there's so much going on, so much passion being thrown out there, that my motto is, DON'T RULE ANYTHING OUT.

Gay men have been very supportive of me over the last couple of years, and lately I've been getting a lot of positive reactions from lesbians, too. When I go to a gay bar, it's not quite as mellow as it used to be, because so many people come up and tell me they appreciate my willingness to stick up for gay rights. But I don't mind the extra attention, because I really enjoy hanging out with gays. They've been through so much that a lot of them are fearless, and they'll do and say anything.

There's this one place I go to in Chicago called Manhole, a little bar with TV screens all around that show the most explicit guy-on-guy porno flicks imaginable. Then there's a back room with a dance floor and a big-screen TV that takes up an entire wall. When you see the pornos on the big screen, it's wild, because the guys' dicks are bigger than life-size. I'm sure a lot of people would be grossed-out by Manhole, but the vibe is great. People don't give a fuck what you look like, and most of the clientele are creative and interesting. It just feels very free and very loose, and I don't feel threatened at all.

I LIKE BEING IN A POSITION TO STICK UP FOR GAY PEOPLE. They're the last ones who should be subjected to any shit, because they're getting hit so hard by the AIDS epidemic. AIDS is such a scary disease, and the worst part is that it can be spread by such a pleasurable activity. I wish I could say I'm a saint when it comes to practicing safe sex, but the truth is I'm human. It goes back to what I said earlier about men selling out their principles for sex. **In the heat of the moment, we sometimes make bad decisions.** Condoms cramp a lot of people's style, including mine, and there are times when I just roll the dice. If it's someone I know and feel close to, I won't wear a rubber. I think if you're comfortable with your mate, after a while you can do without the miniature raincoat. At times I've had unprotected sex with people I don't really know. But the responsible thing to do in that situation is to always wear a condom, because it's not just your own life that's at stake. If you're a young person, look at it this way: Think of all the SEX you're going to have in this life, AS LONG AS YOU STAY CLEAN. Why would you want to jeopardize that?

I'm not a role model, but I am someone who's in a position to show that sexual identity isn't as absolute as it's made out to be. Our society is so repressed that tens of thousands of gay people have to hide in the closet because the backlash against them is brutal. And it's no coincidence that you almost never hear about any openly gay athletes, especially in the four major pro sports leagues—the NBA, NFL, NHL, and Major League Baseball. There are a lot of gay athletes, but the sports world is the ultimate prison of macho bullshit, so nobody knows who these people are. I hope I can help to break down the walls of hatred, ignorance, and bigotry.

It's a big joke to a lot of people right now, but maybe as time passes the laughter will grow quieter and quieter.

Twelve

Worship at the Church of Love

***W**hen I die, I want to be stripped naked, frozen, and placed in a see-through freezer.* I want to be put on display—in my house, or maybe in some sort of museum—so people can come by and check me out forevermore.

I'll have a smile on my face, and there will be tape recordings of my voice for the onlookers to hear. I'll say things like, "Oh people, I know you're sitting there watching me and just tripping out. Imagine how stupid you look right now, looking at someone who's dead. Now get a life and go home."

There will be all kinds of funky comments: "Hey, sweet thing, I'm looking at you right now, and you've got a nice ass." Or: "Yo, big man, you've got some crusty shit under your nose." It will freak people out and make them laugh about a subject that almost everyone is scared to confront. Besides, it's the closest I'll ever come to immortality, because my heart damn sure won't beat forever.

I spend a lot of time thinking about death. **I've thought about suicide and I've thought about murder,** though neither is very likely to happen. The odds of me murdering someone, unless it's in self-defense, are about the same as the odds of me getting a job on Wall Street. **I DREAM ABOUT DEATH, AND DIFFERENT**

WAYS OF DYING, PRACTICALLY EVERY NIGHT.

Some people think that I'm obsessed with death, or that I have a death wish. Not really. I figure the only way to handle death is to make it a part of your reality and realize that it can happen at any time. If you look at it that way, every waking moment is precious, and every action is lasting. That doesn't mean your day-to-day existence has to be heavy and somber. It's not like the Grim Reaper is waiting to snatch you up. If anything, the inevitability of death should be an excuse to be loose and have fun.

I'm not afraid of death. I'm not afraid of getting killed. One day I'm gonna be dead, anyway. If I go out a little earlier than planned, so be it. Whatever happens, happens. Death might be right around the corner, but I'm not going to live my life in fear.

SEVERAL YEARS AGO, I CAME SO CLOSE TO DYING IT WAS UNBELIEVABLE.

I was visiting a friend and he took me to this black club. I knew something was up, but I figured I'd just keep my mouth shut, as long as he didn't do anything sketchy in front of me.

Well, things got sketchy, all right. We were in this club and all of a sudden a dude whips out a gun and starts shooting at my friend. **I WAS STANDING *RIGHT NEXT TO* THE GUY, AND BULLETS ARE FLYING, AND I COULDN'T FUCKING BELIEVE IT.** I thought I was gonna die for sure. We took off running across the club and got to the front door, and then I stopped. I thought to myself, "What the hell am I doing?" They were shooting at him, not me, so I let him go and got the hell out of that neighborhood. It's amazing neither one of us got hit, but I'll never forget that pit I felt in my stomach when I heard that gun go off.

If I had died that night, I would have missed out on a hell of a lot. As much as anyone, I know how fleeting life is and how suddenly things can turn around. You never know what's gonna happen, so you might as well try to stay alive as long as you can. This came up during a conversation I had one night last summer with a little kid who approached me at the Mirage Casino. The boy walked up to me and said, **"I CAME ALL THE WAY HERE TO TELL YOU I'M READY TO KILL MYSELF."** Then he told me that I had saved his life in the past because I had shown him it was okay to be different and to stand up for what you believe in. But now he was so depressed and desperate that he didn't want to live.

My reaction? I guess you could say I gave him tough love. I told him, "Look, this is the way it is. If you want to kill yourself, go ahead, but we're still gonna go on without you and have a great time. No one's gonna give a shit that you're gone, and you'll be the one missing out. You're not bettering yourself in any way by committing suicide, and who knows what you might be missing. Look at me—I was a homeless janitor who could have said he had nothing to live for, and now I'm a huge celebrity. You just never know how things are gonna turn out, so you might as well stick around."

This might not have been the most tender approach, but I

definitely got his attention, and I think he saw my point. We talked for a long time, and by the end of the conversation I at least think he was willing to give life a chance for a while longer. And talking to him made me think about my own mortality and all the things I'd like to experience before I go.

Ideally, I'll die when I'm used up—physically, mentally, and emotionally. And I might as well die with nothing in my pockets. I'd like for my daughter to be taken care of, but other than that, ***they can take any cash I have left and use it to throw a huge party celebrating my death.*** Because, who really knows what dying means? **MAYBE DEATH IS LIKE THE ETERNAL OR-GASM.** Maybe it makes life look lame. Maybe people don't come back from the dead because there's no way in hell they'd ever want to. Maybe it's like a basketball player going from San Antonio to Chicago, then wanting to go back to playing for the Spurs. It's just not going to happen.

Whatever death is, the fact that I know it's coming is almost comforting, because it keeps me from taking a lot of the shit going on in my life too seriously. `I'll die by myself, probably solo in the bedroom, and I'm fine with that.` I can't take my friends or the people that I love the most with me, so I know that in life I can't rely on them for fulfillment. **PEACE HAS TO COME FROM WITHIN,** and I wasn't able to achieve it until a few years ago, when `I STOPPED LIVING A LIE AND STARTED LIS-TENING TO MY INNER BEING`. I was fed up with trying to be the good soldier, the perfect American athlete, and it got to the point where I sat alone in my pickup truck in an empty parking lot in middle of the night and put a gun in my lap. I was so pained by the life of kissing ass and restraint I had forged that I considered blowing my head off. Instead, I decided to kill the person who was trying to conform to everyone else's standards.

Now I know I'm going to die happy, because I've traveled such a long road to self-discovery and fulfillment. I've been homeless and hungry. I've been an airport janitor who was arrested for stealing watches from a gift shop. I've been funny-looking and criminally shy. I've lived with a white family in an Oklahoma town where people routinely called me "nigger" and threw rocks at my car as I drove by. I've endured pain and hardship and the fear of being just another nobody, and I survived the make-believe existence I created based on other people's expectations. Then I lived with my foot on the gas pedal and kept myself open to new experiences, and I crossed paths with a lot of my fellow space-travelers who were interesting as shit. I have high standards, but I'm not a perfectionist. **IF I DROP DEAD TODAY, THEN IT'S A GREAT DAY. MY LIFE HAS BEEN ONE BIG ORGY OF LOVE, PAIN, JOY, PASSION, SADNESS, ANGER, EXCITEMENT, AND SURPRISE.** I was a 5-11 bum who sprouted up to 6-8 two years after high school—and somehow, I made it all the way to the top. When I go, please don't mourn.

SCREAM AT THE TOP OF YOUR LUNGS WITH GLEE, AND HOPEFULLY I'LL SEND THAT LOVE BACK TO YOU FROM THE GREAT BEYOND.

That's basically the way I reacted when my old friend from Oklahoma, Don (Duck) Taylor, died a few years ago. Duck was probably the closest person to me who has ever died—I've been really lucky that way—and the way I reacted was strange. I felt bad, but I couldn't really be sorry because he was the ultimate live-for-the-moment, good-time dude. Duck knew for years that he probably wouldn't live that long because of his bad heart, so he lived with abandon and without regret. **I know he would've hated the thought of us moping around at his funeral, SO WE SHOWED UP READY TO CELEBRATE.**

When Duck died, I was playing for the Spurs but was on the suspended list because we were battling over my contract. So I was in Vegas with Billy Penz when we got the news, and we didn't have much time to get back to Bokchito. We raced to the airport and flew to Dallas and then got a limo to pick up Bryne Rich and haul ass up to Oklahoma. We got to the funeral right as it was starting and we must have looked pretty funny: we weren't wearing black suits or anything like that, just jeans and Chuck Taylors. Most of the people knew me from way back so they didn't freak out when I showed up. I really wasn't paying too much attention to the ceremony, but once it ended I had to celebrate. **IT WAS LIKE A DAMN MARDI GRAS. I HAD TO CELEBRATE BECAUSE DUCK HAD A GREAT LIFE.**

Did Duck go to heaven? Couldn't tell you, bro. What's funny is how everyone trips out on what happens after death, but no one really stresses about what might have happened before, as if our energy never existed before this lifetime. If time is endless, then shouldn't the great beyond extend equally in both directions? `I believe that I've been alive before, specifically as a shark—A GREAT WHITE SHARK,` even though I'm black in this life. I have no concrete evidence, but I can feel it in my soul. I like to attack shit, and it seems like something that's been with me for a long, long time.

I don't know what happens after you die, but `I think the whole idea of a day of reckoning is bullshit.` That's just propaganda designed to get people to kiss ass and live scared. **WHAT I BELIEVE IN IS KARMA.** Good energy is recycled, and so is negative energy. That doesn't mean there's some big scoreboard that decides which way you're headed for eternity, based on how you acted. And the energy might not come back at you directly. But *the more good energy that people put out there, the better things will be, and vice versa.*

The whole idea that you will pay for your sins is put out there by religions that want to run your life. So is the notion that the afterlife is what's really important. If you buy into that, you can also be sold the notion that what happens during your life on earth is meaningless—and that's a dangerous mentality. This is how a lot of wars are sold to the masses in places like the Middle East. They convince these poor people whose lives are so bleak that they might as well sacrifice everything for God so that they can be rewarded in the afterlife. Why would anyone possibly take that bet? Life is life, and for all we know it's everything. *YOU CAN PRAY ALL YOU WANT, BUT YOU'D BETTER TRY TO MAKE THE BEST OF YOUR SITUATION INSTEAD OF COUNTING ON SOMEONE ELSE'S IDEA OF ETERNAL BLISS.*

I'm a very spiritual person, but I think the organized religions that are out there are too controlling to handle my far-out beliefs. I don't believe in God. I BELIEVE IN WHAT I CALL THE HOLY SPIRIT. People are raised to believe that God is this cure-all for their problems, and that carries over into their adult lives. Whenever people are in trouble or in danger, they'll all of a sudden turn to God for help, as if it's that simple. I have to admit I'm the same way. I'm very religious when shit is wrong, but I have only a mild religious belief when things are going along well.

Does that mean I rely on God to get me out of a jam? Hell, no. *If there is a supreme being, he/she/it has a hell of a lot more to worry about than my stupid problems.* I don't look at it that way at all. What I believe is that the Holy Spirit lives within all of us, and when you turn to it, what you're really doing is trying to summon the strength within yourself. If you want to love God, then love the God within yourself and within others, and love will shine back upon you. It's not like you have to follow some strict set of religious guidelines. **JUST FOLLOW WHAT YOU KNOW IS RIGHT IN YOUR HEART.**

Spirituality is such a complex, heavy concept that people try to simplify it to make sense of it. They just lay it all on God as the explanation for everything. I mean, no one on earth knows or has seen God. They can probably feel the vibes and the energy and the electrical impulse that's coming through their bodies and making them feel a certain way. Some inner/outer dimension is in there doing something, making them do and feel certain things. Something's going on in there, and it makes people feel better to just say it's God and not take responsibility for the energy inside.

When I pray, I don't ask the Holy Spirit for anything, I just do a lot of soul-searching and try to get in touch with my spirituality. I pray every single day that I can withstand all the turmoil and trials and tribulation. The Holy Spirit provides us with strength, and it needs to be nurtured. **WHEN EDDIE VEDDER SINGS, IT'S COMING FROM HIS SOUL, AND THAT'S HOW HE ALLOWS THE HOLY SPIRIT INSIDE OF HIM TO COME OUT.**

For me, prayer is a way to filter out all the bullshit that's thrown in my face and to remind myself what is real and what is holy.

I was force-fed religion as a kid. My mother, a Southern Baptist, was a church organist for forty years, and I had no choice but to go. So twice every Sunday, I went to the Church of Living God in the Oak Cliff area of Dallas, where I grew up. I learned the Bible inside out, and I still remember most of it. I didn't question having to go twice a day at first, but when I got a little older I started to reject all of the rules and got sick of being told what to do. So finally I told my mom, "I don't want to go to church; I want to watch football this Sunday. I want to watch the Cowboys." Eventually I just stopped going to church, and my mother understood. I'd still go every so often, and she didn't try to push me any further on the issue. You don't have to be in CHURCH to feel your SPIRITUALITY.

One day late in the summer of 1995 I showed up at the Church of Living God on the spur of the moment. When I walked in people were all whispering, and then the preacher saw me and said, "We'd like to thank our Brother Rodman for joining us again after being away from the church for so long." Some people looked at me like I was the Brother From Another Planet. Others remembered me from when I was a little boy. All of them rose when the preacher made that announcement and gave me a standing ovation.

Spirituality is important to me. I look at prayer or going to church or times of religious contemplation as ways for me to protect and cherish my inner soul. I go a lot of places and take a lot of chances and expose so much—on a number of levels—but there has to be something that I keep to myself, that's untouchable. **The INNER SOUL is what I protect and SHIELD WITH ALL MY WILL. It's like the core of a rattler, and I will strike if anyone or anything gets too close or tries to mess with it.** The only person who has ever seen it is my daughter, Alexis, and that's because there's a cosmic bond and trust between us that allows us to connect on that sacred level.

I can't tell you too much about my inner soul. What's in there is my business. I will say that it's like a roller coaster, with twists and turns and thrills and spills and falls that make your stomach drop. But that doesn't mean it's unsettled in there. *All of it grooves together and allows me to shine.*

The inner soul is where I house my notions of right and wrong and good and evil. Some of those values are obvious, like the one that tells me it's wrong to kill or harm another human—with some exceptions. **IF YOU HAVE TO KILL SOMEONE, IF THEY'RE FUCKING WITH YOUR CHILD OR FAMILY, IF THERE ARE NO OTHER OPTIONS, THEN YOU'RE GOING TO DO WHAT YOU HAVE TO DO.** Every day, hundreds of people kill each other in the name of their countries or religions. And there are war zones all over America, with people dying for gangs or drugs or just looking the wrong way. I don't want to add to all of the murder in society. **IF YOU TRY TO HURT ME OR MY DAUGHTER, I'LL TAKE YOU OUT, BUT I WON'T WANT TO.** And if it's a choice between killing and damaging a person, I'll just try to damage them.

I have respect for life and respect for the dead. ***The other night a woman wanted to do me in a graveyard—or should I say a boneyard—and I turned her down.*** That's a line that even I won't cross, one of the very few lines I won't cross. But the whole idea spooks me a little, because **SEX IS SUCH AN AFFIRMATION OF LIFE, AND I DON'T WANT TO THROW IT IN THE FACE OF THE DEAD.**

DON'T FUCK IN A CEMETERY is one of my Ten Commandments. Now, don't get me wrong. I'm not God or Moses. I'm not big on telling people what to do. **I JUST HAVE SOME IDEAS ON HOW TO MAKE THIS WORLD A BETTER PLACE FOR ALL OF US, AND YOU CAN FOLLOW THEM IF YOU'D LIKE.**

Many people who are really into religion are just looking for something to fill a void in their lives, and I have no problem with that. As long as you keep your perspective and realize that the Holy Spirit lives within all of us, I think it's fine. As much as I hate the idea of having to follow rules, and as much as the heavy-handedness of many religions bugs me, I'm all for the concept of forgiveness that many religions promote.

I'm a forgiving person, loyal to a fault, even when people aren't loyal to me. I'M LOYAL TO EVERYBODY I LOVE—my daughter, my relatives, my friends, and my lovers. I may not call or be there for them every day or every week, but I'm loyal. If they need anything, I'm there. If they need a shoulder to cry on or someone to lean on, I'm there. That's me, because heaven knows I've needed that a million times before.

The only time I ever turn my back on people is if they fuck me over first or stab me in the back. **ONE TIME I GOT SHAFTED OUT OF $50,000 BY A GUY WHO I THOUGHT WAS MY FRIEND.** I was helping him fund a basketball camp and he invested the money and lost it. That was pretty brutal, and, as you might imagine, it was too difficult for us to stay friends after that.

But most of the time when I get fucked over by someone I give that person one more chance, even two more chances. Even all the women who fuck me over and lie to me, I'll still give them another chance. Not because I want to go back and fuck them, or have some type of relationship with them. It's just that I believe I have to be better than the situation, rise above it and do what's right. **Everyone makes mistakes. I've made tons of mistakes and people have forgiven me, so I try to do the same for others.**

To me, forgiveness, loyalty, sin, morality, death, spirituality, and religion are all intertwined. If Alexis asks me about religion, I'll tell her this: Always Keep The Holy Spirit In

THE TEN COMMANDMENTS

1. Thou shalt not fake an orgasm.
2. Thou shalt not release flatulence during sex.
3. Thou shalt douche before being eaten.
4. Thou shalt not talk too much in the morning.
5. Thou shalt not fuck in a cemetery.
6. Thou shalt not ask another man to fuck one's wife.
7. Thou shalt not rise in the middle of sexual intercourse and defecate.
8. Thou shalt not name-drop.
9. Thou shalt love thyself frequently.
10. Thou shalt worship at the Church of Love

You, Believe In What You Believe In, And Ask For His Forgiveness If You Feel You've Done Something Wrong. That's it. **NO FASTING, NO CONFESSION, NO GUILT, AND NO SACRIFICE.** We face enough pressures in this life without trying to figure out the way some god wants us to behave.

If there's one way we can improve our world and our individual realities, it's to **WORSHIP AT THE CHURCH OF LOVE. THE CHURCH IS WITHIN YOU, AND THE LOVE IS WHAT RULES YOUR SPIRIT**—what some people call god. Love is a word that gets thrown around too casually, and to be honest, I don't actually know the true definition. But I do know what love isn't: Ownership, for one thing. **A lot of people, when they say, "I LOVE YOU," are really saying, "I OWN YOU."** They take their connection with a person and call it love, and then they think that gives them the right to run that person's life.

Love is something you can't force. A lot of people have fucked-up relationships and try to stick it out in the name of love. The only way they can keep the relationship going is if they have sex and say, "I love you, baby" all the time. Sex has a little bit to do with love, and love can have a lot to do with sex if the vibe is right. But mostly I think the two concepts get confused.

When I watch a movie or TV show and see a man getting all soft and moist with a woman, it drives me absolutely nuts. I have to turn it off, because to me it's torture, like fingernails on blackboards. I'll see someone say, "Oh baby, I love you soooo much," and it just seems so superficial. There's nothing wrong with expressing your love for someone, but you can do it without surrendering your dignity. As much as I encourage men to show their feminine side, this is like a pet-peeve issue for me. When I see a guy cooing to his woman, I see him as weak—very weak. I'm not saying he's not a man, I'm just saying he's a weak man, at least at that moment. You can say you love a woman and still be firm and direct, but I can't tell you how many times I've seen guys just crumble to pieces in front of their women, and it makes my stomach turn.

There are a lot of people that are pussy-whipped, and, for that matter, there are a lot of dick-whipped women (and men), too. That goes back to people using sex as love. **THE WORLD IS CONTROLLED BY SEX. PEOPLE FEEL THEY'VE GOT TO HAVE THAT PUSSY OR THAT DICK, AND THEY'LL DO ANYTHING TO GET IT, EVEN ACT LIKE A FOOL IN PUBLIC.** I think when you're saying you love somebody a lot, it means that you're trying to find out what that word really means.

LOVE IS A FOUR-LETTER WORD that makes people feel so sensitive, so emotional, so fragile, and so careful. It's a heavy, heavy word, and in our society it usually goes hand-in-hand with monogamy. If you love someone and they love you, neither of you is supposed to sleep with someone else. It's a twisted idea in some ways, and in this day and age I don't think it's very realistic. ***I believe that you can have a soul mate, but it doesn't mean that you're the only two people for each other in the history of the world.***

A lot of people meet someone they think is their perfect mate and then they stop searching for other potential lovers. That's the whole monogamy thing, and I think that limits people's experiences and locks them into relationships that may not actually be perfect. **IF YOU'RE LOOKING FOR TRUE LOVE, MAKE SURE YOUR SEARCH IS BROAD.** It can take a lifetime to find your ideal mate. You have to try to have as many experiences as you can. YOU CAN'T JUST FIND ONE PERSON AND SAY, "THIS IS MY LOVE." THERE'S NO WAY IN HELL YOU CAN DO THAT. A lot of people get married two or three times—"I love you, I love you, I love you"—but I couldn't fool myself like that.

Look at me—I got together with my ex-wife, had a baby, then decided well after the fact that marriage was worth trying. Back then I was just dazed. I liked her in the beginning, but I didn't love her. After the baby came there was something there, but we got married for the wrong reason. We just weren't compatible. It was more like an obligation—you have to get married for Alexis—and that put it all on the child, which made it even worse when we broke up.

My ex-girlfriend Stacy was as close to a

soul mate as I've found. We had the same vibe, a lot of the same chemistry. We also had a crazy sexual energy between us that led to some wild experiences. She and I could have gone all over the world together as soul mates. We sort of viewed things from the same place. But we're not together anymore. It's one of those deals where she has her own thing going and I have my own thing going. Who knows whether we'll be together in the future. If it happens, it happens. If it doesn't, it doesn't. In the meantime, of the women I've been with, I still haven't found anyone I connect with quite like her. My general feeling is, **you don't love the women you go out with, because it just fucks things up.** They start taking everything too seriously, and then you have nothing to look forward to later in life.

There are a lot of people in this world I love—my close friends, my mom and my sisters; and, of course, my daughter. There are many different kinds of love. With your mom and your sisters, you hope nothing happens to them and hope everything goes right for them, but it's not like they're always in your thoughts. A good friend is someone you can keep forever, so you love that person for what you've been through together and for being there in good times and bad.

IF I HAD TO TRULY BREAK IT DOWN, I HAVE ONLY ONE TRUE LOVE, AND THAT'S ALEXIS. My love for her is so strong, so raw that I can't describe it. If someone was shooting at her I would

I'D GIVE ALEXIS ANYTHING . . .

step in front of her and take the bullet without even thinking about it. That's a no-brainer, I'd have no choice. I think the only true love you can have is for your kids. You can end a relationship with your mate but you can never break up with your child.

To me, being a parent is the ultimate power and the ultimate challenge. Of all the magical wonders of this earth, a person's child is by far the most sacred.

Thirteen

Be
Your
Own
Authority
Figure

wo weeks after the murder of Nicole Brown Simpson and Ronald Goldman, *I paid a visit to O.J.'s house on Rockingham Drive in Brentwood and interrogated the only eyewitness to the crime.* It was right after the '93–94 season had ended, and I was in L.A. hanging out with Bryne Rich and Jack Haley. We were as caught up in the drama as everyone else. I had met O.J. a couple of times before, and there had been so much bullshit circulating about who had done what to whom and when, and I decided I'd do a little investigating on my own.

So Jack, Bryne, and I just drove over there and walked up past the police barricades, and the people outside O.J.'s house recognized me. They went in and got his son, Jason. He seemed pretty happy to see me—I guess he's a basketball fan—and he invited us inside.

That's when I decided to put my detective skills to work. While Jack and Bryne were talking to Jason and checking out the house, I went and found Kato—not Kato Kaelin, the wanna-be-celebrity, but Kato, the Akita who was at Nicole's house at the time of the murders.

Most people can't talk to dogs, but I have a bond with the canine tribe. My German shepherds, Aran and Katy, are communicative as hell, and I talk to them, though I'm usually telling them not to eat my friends. Most dogs are great communicators, and most of them are a lot smarter than people think. So I walked right up to Kato and asked him what was going on, but he wouldn't tell me anything.

I tried hitting him with some direct questions, but the dog didn't say shit. He just barked up a storm. If I had known what canine language he was speaking I would've figured it out. But I was pretty sure the dog was holding out on me, so I gave up and asked Jason what really happened.

When I want to know something, I don't rely on gossip, press coverage, or the system to provide me with the answers. My thing is, whenever possible, **GO STRAIGHT TO THE SOURCE.** Most people care more about maintaining their own kingdoms than they do about the truth, anyway. I'm not one of those suckers who believes what the people in power want me to believe. I want to find things out for myself.

So I said to Jason, `"OK, tell me what really happened. Did your father kill her or what?"` He said, "No dude." I mean, he was protecting his father, which is normal. I could tell he didn't want to talk about it. So we just hung out around the house for about an hour. There were some other people there—O.J.'s sisters, I think, and some friends—but I didn't bother asking anyone besides Jason and the dog if O.J. did it.

The only thing left to do was to ask O.J. himself. I thought about visiting him in jail but I never got it together because I left town pretty soon after I went to his house. O.J. and I have only met a couple of times, once at a game and once when we were out somewhere. Both times we talked, and he seemed pretty down to earth. If I ever see him again, I'll still ask him, straight-out, if he killed Nicole and Ron Goldman. But so much shit has gone on by now that I don't think he'd tell me.

The whole O.J. saga showed how messed up the power structure is in our society. You had black people who knew in their hearts that O.J. probably did it, but they were rooting for him to get off because they're so sick of getting shafted and framed by racist cops who think they're God just because they've got a badge. You had white people who are so out of touch with the way things go down on the streets and in the courts that they thought blacks were just paranoid and Mark Fuhrman was a to-tal fluke. You had media outlets falling all over each other to re-port facts that weren't necessarily true. You had race, sex, power, and money, and **the BOTTOM LINE IS a GUY PROB-ABLY GOT AWAY WITH MURDER BECAUSE HE WAS RICH.**

If I ever kill anyone, remind me to hire Johnnie Cochran and Robert Shapiro and Barry Scheck and to buy all the expert testi-mony I can possibly afford. By the time those lawyers got through with their arguments, you couldn't even be sure the shoes on O.J.'s feet were actually his. Johnnie Cochran sold his soul to make everyone believe that O.J. didn't do it. That's his job. And then after he and everybody else sold their souls, they sold their stories to make even more money.

By the time the O.J. trial came to a close, it was so muddled and impossible to follow that I figured he'd probably get off. I think a lot of people thought so, too. I remember watching the verdict from Dwight Manley's house in Southern California and I was not surprised. When the verdict came down I was happy—not because O.J. got off but because the damn thing was finally over. Maybe that's what the jurors were thinking, too. By that point, it didn't matter if he was guilty or not—just get the damn thing out of the way. People were living their lives for that trial. It was time to move on.

The O.J. case was interesting, and it's possible a man got away with murder. But that shit happens every day, and no one even pays any attention. **A lot of the black people who cheered when O.J. got acquitted were just happy a brother finally beat the system after so many others have been beaten down by it.** As a black man, I can see why someone would mistrust authority. We all have to deal with authority, every day, and sometimes it can drive you insane.

So many people think they're authority figures when they're not. They have some stupid power over you, like whether you can go through a certain door or what you can wear to get into a restaurant, and they'll do anything they can to make you feel that power. Assholes like this are everywhere—on TV, on the streets, and definitely at the workplace—and if you try to fight each and every one of them, you'll explode.

Instead of battling every idiot on a power trip, I try to pick my spots. Some people earn my respect, like Chuck Daly or Phil

Jackson, but my general rule is not to recognize anyone's authority, except your parents' when you're growing up. Beyond that, ***no one can run your life for you but you.*** People who think they're in charge of you can tell you what to do, and you can follow their rules to make your life easier. But you don't have to accept those rules. The best thing is to BE YOUR OWN AUTHORITY FIGURE. In the end, you have to decide in your heart when to go along with authority and when to make a stand. Ask yourself whether what they're telling you to do makes sense, and you decide if it's worth doing. There are times when you'll have to hold your tongue, but as long as you don't get mind-fucked by the people trying to push you around—as long as you're the one in control of your soul—you won't be anybody's puppet.

You should Follow The Law Of Your Soul, even if it contradicts the law of the land. I respect the legal system in America to a point. The law seems to have a way of taking shit into its own hands, just because it can flash a badge and a gun. Some cops have this attitude that says, "Hey, I'm the police. I can fuck with you totally, twice over." That's what the whole Mark Fuhrman thing was about. **WHITE PEOPLE THINK THE IDEA OF HIM PLANTING EVIDENCE WAS A JOKE, BUT BLACKS KNOW THAT SHIT HAPPENS ALL THE TIME.** There are two legal systems in the United States, one for whites and one for blacks. I've definitely felt like I'm treated differently by some cops because I'm black, so I know people who are poor and aren't celebrities must get it a lot worse. I still get stopped by cops for no reason, but they let me go when they realize who I am. That's kind of fucked up, but that's the way the world works, and the world is a fucked up place.

Then again, some cops have a hard-on for me because I'm rich and famous. One evening in January of 1997 I was with two friends of mine cruising around Chicago in my truck. We were on our way to a surprise party for my friend Larry at a bar, and we parked the truck on a residential street so Larry wouldn't see it when he drove up. Well, we were the ones who got the surprise. The truck was parked and the engine was off when this cop walked by with a newspaper and a bag of donuts. He had left his partner, who was writing up a speeding ticket a couple of blocks away, and went off to run an errand, which is the only reason he saw the truck. He noticed the license plate

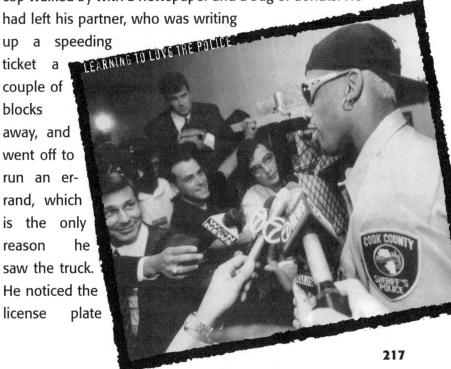

didn't have the correct markings—it was supposed to be a special truck tag—so he asked me to get out of the truck and show him some registration. No big deal, but **THIS COP WAS BUSTING MY BALLS ALL THE WAY.** He asked to see my driver's license, but he was pissing me off, so I told him I didn't have it with me. He said, "Well, how do I know who you are?"—which was total bullshit, because he later made a comment to his captain about how I make $9 million a year and ought to be able to afford the right license plate.

Anyway, **the cop wanted to prove to me that he was in command, and I wouldn't go along with it**, so we played this stupid cat-and-mouse game out there on the street in the freezing cold. He told me that since I didn't have my license, I would have to come down to the station. "Can't you just call in my name and find out whether my license is valid?" I asked him. "Isn't that what you normally do?" He insisted that I come down to the station, and I said, "For what? Either write me a ticket or leave." He told me that technically I was under arrest. "For what?" I asked. Finally, I showed him my license, but he still wasn't satisfied. He made me follow him all the way across town to the police station because I had the wrong license plate and because my windows were tinted.

Would this have happened if I was just some guy on the street? Of course not. *I WAS THIS COP'S TROPHY, HIS WAY OF PROVING HIS MANHOOD.* The absurd thing was that once we walked into the station all of the people there were all over me asking for autographs and hugs and shit. Another cop brought out this young boy who had run away and had him shake my hand. The cop went back to talk about the situation with his captain, and the captain basically told him to mellow out. My bodyguard, George, is an off-duty Chicago cop, and he came down to the station and told the other officers that the car was registered in his name and that if anyone was gonna get a ticket, it should be him. Finally we got to leave and we headed back to the restaurant for the party. This time, we parked on the main boulevard and walked across the street. Before we got to the door, Larry walked up. "Hey," he said, "what are you doing here?" Surprise!

It seems like **_people on power trips are naturally drawn to me. It's like I'm the tiger and they have to prove they can tame me._** As much as I love to work, I hate working for people who try to push me around. We all have to deal with bosses who can be pains in the ass. I wasn't happy with the way the Bulls' treated Phil Jackson after Phil won his fourth NBA title. So I bought him the Harley to show that I appreciated what he'd done.

But what about all the people who need to stay at their jobs to make a living? Say your boss is a miserable, fucked-up human being, but you want the job, so you have to deal with the situation. That's a tough call, but here's how I'd handle it: Do what you have to do to stay employed, but **NEVER KISS ANYBODY'S ASS.** I'd tell that boss, "Hey, you're acting all fucked up lately. I need this job, and that's the only reason why I'm here." My boss would have to deal with that, because I wouldn't give him the satisfaction of quitting. If it became too much to bear, then he'd have to fire me. Otherwise, I might end up kicking his ass.

It's not always easy to balance the need to make a living with the need to be your own person. You have to be mentally strong enough to follow someone's orders without giving in to the slave mentality. Even if you're getting paid a shitload of money, some-

DRESS HOW YOU LIKE

times it's just not worth it. Take the fashion industry—that whole scene is filled with so much bullshit, I don't see how people can even walk down the runways. I respect fashion models for the shit they have to put up with. They have to work with assholes and sacrifice their whole livelihood and their health just so they can fit into someone else's idea of what's beautiful and what looks good. I think it's fucked up, and I think the people who run the industry are a bunch of weaklings, but if that's what the models want to do to make a living, they have to take it.

I've been in the projects, and I've been around rich people, so I can see things from both sides.

Back when I was younger, I stole things all the time. It's not like I was breaking into houses. In the projects, the best way to get shot is to bust into someone else's place. You go into somebody's house in the projects, your ass is dead. My friends and I would steal things from 7-Eleven all the time. We'd stick food underneath our clothes. And that's how we'd get new clothes, too. This was before the high-tech days of sensor tags and stuff like that. Back then you could just try on clothes and wear them underneath the clothes you wore in. You could walk right out of the store and not get detected.

Later, when I lived in Bokchito, **I got into stealing car batteries and selling them for quick cash.** In the trunk of my car I used to carry around a wrench with a swiveling head that had half-inch and 9/16 of an inch settings which made for easy battery theft. The thrill was part of it, but it was mostly about making extra cash.

I often wonder whether I've really kicked the habit. If all of a sudden I was back in Oak Cliff with no money, I could see myself turning to crime. It's more likely I'd work at McDonald's or find an honest way to make money, but I can't say for sure. **BEING IN THAT ATMOSPHERE MAKES YOU**

WANT TO BE BAD. There's no other escape that you can visualize, and you feel this need to do something that's productive. **YOU FEEL LIKE SOCIETY IS FUCKING YOU OVER, AND SOMETIMES CRIME MAKES MORE SENSE THAN BANGING YOUR HEAD AGAINST THE WALL FOR FIVE BUCKS AN HOUR.**

On the other side of things, I think I'd be a pretty cool boss. So many CEOs and people like that are cutthroat assholes only looking out for themselves. Why be that way? If I was in charge of a company, I'd give everyone a paid vacation anywhere in the world they want to go, for two weeks every year. They could take their family and just go chill out somewhere, and I'd pay for the whole damn thing. It would be an expensive policy, but morale would be so much better that you'd get your money back with better quality and better production. But even if it didn't end up making money for the company, it would still be the right thing to do, and you'd have more respect and loyalty from your employees.

Another policy I'd have is that you could come to work any way you want. You could dress in shorts or jeans or whatever, as long as you produce. If you're doing your job, that's the main thing. Who gives a shit about the way you look or any of that other bullshit? Companies that make you wear suits are just trying to assert their power over you. I know the feeling—the NBA makes me wear a uniform, too. When you break it down, people telling you what to wear is like them branding you as a slave.

THE ONLY TIME IN LIFE YOU DEFINITELY HAVE TO PUT UP WITH RULES YOU MIGHT

NOT BELIEVE IN IS WHEN YOU'RE A KID. Even though parents sometimes pull power trips, it usually comes from the fact that they care. You have to give them the benefit of the doubt most of the time because they've been through shit that you haven't, like dealing with asshole bosses. Unfortunately, I didn't really have as much parental guidance as I would have liked when I was growing up. **Often, my mom was just too busy working and going to church to deal with me, and my dad was long gone.** It's scary, but I didn't have any authority figures as a kid that I listened to or respected. No teachers, no coaches, no aunts or uncles—nobody. I was just sort of off in my own world, taking it all in. Somehow, I was a decent student, especially when it came to English. I loved my English classes, because they gave me a

MY MOM . . . THE ONLY PERSON I EVER LISTEN TO

chance to be creative. I wish I could have developed my writing skills and worked at it, but there was no one there to push me or guide me, and I just sort of drifted along.

I hope my daughter, Alexis, has more options and guidance than I did. Even though I don't get to see her that often, I think I'm a pretty good parent. I'd like to have custody of her, because she's the one thing in life I really worry about, and I want to be around her.

All kids tell white lies, but I'd stress the importance of telling the truth to Alexis the best I could. I wouldn't be a strict parent, and I'd make it easy for her to appreciate things. But I'd want her to appreciate the value of hard work, because the best way to get your priorities in order is to **WORK FOR WHAT YOU GET. YOU'VE GOT TO WORK, WORK, WORK, WORK, WORK, WORK, WORK.** That's what I did, and I've appreciated what it's got me—I still do. But I wouldn't purposely keep Alexis from enjoying some of the things in life I had to do without. She'd have to work for what she got, but there would be big rewards.

I'd expect Alexis to respect my authority, but I wouldn't be a dictator. Mostly, I'd try to guide her to the right choices and prepare her for adult life, when she has to deal with the same bullshit we all have to deal with. I'd protect her, but I wouldn't shelter her, because no matter what happens there will be people who try to run her life, and I want her to develop a strong sense of survival and of standing up for herself.

After all, life should be a fantastic journey, not a power trip.

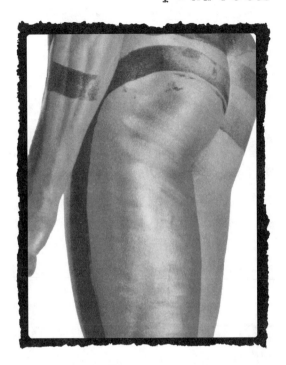

Fourteen

Love It
or
Leave It

*W*hat do Dennis Rodman, Rush Limbaugh, and Jesse Helms have in common?

We've all fantasized about re-ceiving anal sex, and we all love the United States of America.

The first similarity is just an assumption, of course, but I'm dead certain about the second. This country rocks, and I'm sure Rush and Jesse agree.

THE UNITED STATES IS THE GREATEST COUNTRY IN THE WORLD. It's the place that gives you the most freedom—the freedom to speak, the freedom to walk the streets whenever you want, the freedom to go anywhere, *the freedom to call Newt Gingrich a big, hairy ballsack.* Our country is built around independence. In most countries you're very restricted. Once you're born they've already labeled you and figured out what you can and can't do. If you don't go along with their plan, you're a failure. In this country, you can do anything you want to do. If you're successful, great. If you're not successful, great. You get to live on your own and make your own choices.

HOW CAN I NOT BELIEVE IN THE AMERICAN DREAM? I WAS A PISS-

POOR NOBODY LIVING IN THE SLUMS OF DALLAS. I used to crawl five miles through an underground sewage tunnel to sneak into the Texas State Fair. I was an airport janitor who got arrested for stealing watches from a gift shop. I was uneducated, unmotivated, and directionless, and I somehow became a basketball star and entertainment personality. **IF I'M NOT THE AMERICAN DREAM, WHO IS?**

I love the opportunity this country provides, and I love the freedom it protects. But obviously, the USA is not perfect. We all know that racially this is and always has been a fucked-up place. Gay people still don't enjoy equal rights, which is ridiculous. There's too much poverty and hunger and violence, and the people running the country—not the politicians, but the ones pulling the strings—are evil, self-centered assholes.

Politicians are the biggest puppets in the world. They're on power trips, and they'll do anything to keep their power. They'll switch their position in a heartbeat just becase they think it will get them more votes. Some of them start off fighting for what they believe in, but eventually sell their souls. Richard Nixon got caught with Watergate and all that spying and lying, but they're all bad: Reagan, Bush, Clinton, everyone. People say John F. Kennedy had secret deals with all sorts of people, including the mob. I think he was basically trying to get as much pussy as he could. I don't mind a President who tries to get a little action, I just don't think the people we elect are qualified to run the country. The behind-the-scenes bastards, the ones who control the guns and money, have ways of getting to the politicians, and the politicians don't have the juice or the balls to fight them.

Politics in America is all bullshit. It's all based on the three L's—**LIE, LIE, LIE.** Show me a politician, I'll show you a bullshit artist. They're all the same, basically. ***They're white men in suits trying to run the country, even though it's the people around them and the evil white men in the shadows who really run it.*** It's all a masquerade. How else could it be that a B-movie actor, Ronald Reagan, was considered a great president? The behind-the-scenes bastards found a chump to play a part, and he did it for eight years and fooled all the suckers out there. Nancy Reagan probably made more decisions than him. If I met Nancy, I'd say, "Your husband was a great President, how was your love life?" Simple as that. I'd say that to every President's wife. I'd ask, "Are you fucking at all? Are y'all like doing it in the Oval Office?"

I'd ask Hillary Rodman—I mean Rodham—Clinton the same thing. During the 1996 Democratic Convention in Chicago, she used that same joke: that she was Hillary Rodman Clinton. I thought it was funny. I would have gone down there and given her a big kiss in front of everybody if I could have gotten in, but the place was completely sold out. **I WOULD HAVE GIVEN HER A KISS SHE'D NEVER FORGET.** I can't imagine Hillary and Bill having sex. MAYBE IF

SHE WAS WEARING A STRAP-ON DILDO AND DOING HIM FROM BE- HIND, BUT THAT'S ABOUT IT.

I'd rather talk to Hillary than her husband. Bill Clinton is not interesting to me. He lives his life in a glass case. **HE KISSES SERIOUS ASS.** He has no choice. That's his job. ***ON THE OTHER HAND, HE SEEMS TO HAVE HAD SOME HOT WOMEN ON THE SIDE IN HIS EARLY YEARS.*** Good for him. If I were the President, I'd screw some fine fucking secretaries in the White House. Hell, yeah, I'd sample the goods. Gennifer Flowers said in *Penthouse* that Clinton ate pussy like a champ. I'd have a lot more respect for Clinton if he would have said, "Yeah, I screwed around. What the hell? I smoked weed and yes, I inhaled." Don't lie about it and insult everyone's intelligence. **YOU SMOKED IT AND YOU DIDN'T INHALE IT? YEAH, RIGHT.** He's a goddamned liar. There's no way in hell he didn't inhale. You cannot say that. If you're gonna hit a joint, you're gonna hit the shit out of it.

Everyone pays so much attention to the presidency, but if you really look at it, the President is largely a figurehead. The most important role a President plays is to act like he has his shit to- gether during times of national crisis. The people with real power are the Supreme Court Justices. I wish someone like me could get appointed, because then I could get rid of some of the stupid-ass laws this country has. I wouldn't follow any particular political agenda—for example, I'm prochoice and pro-death-penalty. As with my sexuality, I can definitely go both ways.

The first law I'd change would be statutory rape. It's one thing to protect a twelve-year-old girl from fucking a thirty-year-old guy—that's a legitimate law. **But to make it illegal for two seventeen-year-olds to have consensual sex?** That's ridiculous. Kids are having sex these days at twelve or thirteen, and hormones are running wild. I'd probably make the cutoff age sixteen. But I still have a problem with a law that would penalize two fifteen-year-olds who want to have sex with each other. The law would probably be that anyone under sixteen who has sex with someone over twenty-one is in trouble, or something like that.

While we're on the subject, sodomy laws would have to go, too. In some states it's still illegal to have anal sex, even oral sex. If anything, I THINK IT SHOULD BE IL-LEGAL FOR WOMEN NOT TO GIVE HEAD. These laws are only designed to fuck with gay people, and they should be eliminated from the books.

I think the funniest law of all is indecent exposure. Hell, YOU'RE BORN NAKED. HOW COULD IT BE IN-DECENT? I know it grosses some people out to look at certain people's bodies, but most people who want to show their bodies are going to be good-looking. Besides, what kind of logic is that? If we're trying to shield our eyes from scary sights in the buff, does that mean we should outlaw bad polyester shirts, or fat people in general? **PEOPLE SHOULD BE ALLOWED TO DO ANYTHING THEY WANT WITH THEIR BODIES.**

I'd make sure there were more nude beaches in America. They should be public and legal, but people in the United States flip out and can't handle it. In Europe they're much more secure about nudity and their beaches are pretty much all topless. You'll be walking by a health-food store and they'll have an advertisement with a woman who's butt-naked saying, "You can have a body like this." Right on.

Look, I'm not totally insensitive to the prudish elements of our society. For example, *I wouldn't allow unlimited public sex.* I'd put some restrictions on it. You'd have to do it where people would be less nosy, just because people are very anal. Even though it's something natural, I can't make the anal people deal with it, because their structure and image of life is already fucked up.

So here's my law: **IF YOU WANT TO HAVE PUBLIC SEX, GO HAVE SEX IN YOUR CAR. IF YOU WANT A**

ALL EXPOSURE IS DECENT

231

BLOW JOB, GO GET A BLOW JOB IN YOUR CAR. KNOCK YOURSELF OUT. JUST DON'T MAKE IT SO OBVIOUS. DON'T DO IT IN THE PARK WHERE EVERYONE CAN SEE YOU.

I know, I know: I've broken that rule many times, as I admitted earlier in this book. But I never claimed to be a perfect citizen, and you know what they say: Rules are made to be broken.

Two other laws I'd throw out are the ones requiring people to wear motorcycle helmets and seat belts. If you want to wear helmets or seat belts, great. If not, that's your business. It's not hurting anybody but you. Laws like that are just excuses to try to run people's lives.

Even if you don't agree with these changes, the idea of improving our laws shouldn't bother you. **THAT'S ONE OF THE GREAT THINGS ABOUT AMERICANS: WE CAN ADMIT OUR MISTAKES, AND WE'RE OPEN TO PROGRESS.** Just think how fucked up things were in the early days, when slavery was legal. Here we had this country founded on freedom, and people like Thomas Jefferson and George Washington had black men and women as their slaves. That's called being unclear on the concept.

I don't think I would've been a very good slave. I would've got my ass beat a lot. I would've been like the guy from *Roots*, Kunta Kinte, refusing to go by his slave name. I don't think I could be ordered around like that. *I'd probably be the one*

sneaking into the master's house to show his wife what a big, black python between the legs looks like. They'd have had to kill me, or maybe I would've escaped. I have a very strong survival instinct. It's the force behind a lot of what I accomplish on the basketball court—but there's no way I could ever have been that obedient.

Even today, THE BLACK CULTURE STILL HASN'T RECOVERED FROM SLAVERY. You can see it in the poverty, the crime, and the amount of single-parent families. **When you take a proud group of people and whip them and rape them and humiliate them to the point of torture, it's not something they can easily shake off.** White people should understand that, but a lot of them don't, and this is still a very racist country.

Because I have a lot of white friends and date mostly white women, there are some black people, especially women, who give me a hard time. At this one nightspot in Chicago, Martini Ranch, there was this one sister who would get on me about dating black women every time I came in. I don't blame black women for questioning this kind of thing; I can see their point. But my whole perspective is that black women dissed me and dogged me until I was in the NBA, and now all of a sudden they want to date me. At some point people have to realize that it's a free country. I should be allowed to be with whoever I want. I think . . .

...all people are racist in their own way.

It's so obvious. I think many Jewish parents want their kids to marry Jewish people, and that's biased. I think Italians are the same way—as is any culture, really. Everyone wants you to stick with your own. I honestly believe I'm one of the most well adjusted people when it comes to racism because I recognize it, but it breezes right through me. I'm an equal-opportunity carouser. And I don't give a fuck what kind of person my daughter marries. As long as he's nice to her, I don't care what race he is.

I'VE BEEN VICTIMIZED BY RACISM, JUST LIKE ANY BLACK IN AMERICA, BUT I DON'T THINK OF MYSELF AS A VICTIM. People have called me "nigger," "spearchucker," "black motherfucker"—you name it, bro. When I was in college, I'd drive down the street and people would throw rocks and cans and other shit at me. **I CAME SO CLOSE TO PICKING UP A 36-GAUGE SHOTGUN AND BLOWING SOME KU KLUX KLAN-LOVING ASSHOLES' HEAD OFF, BUT LUCKILY I RESTRAINED MYSELF.** I remember many times that Bryne Rich convinced me not to do it, and I'm so thankful. But racism is so deep rooted, it's hard to escape. Even Bryne's mom, who took me into her home and did so much for me, was embarrassed to have me in her car at first, and there were times she would take the back way home so nobody would see me in the car with her. How is that supposed to make a young man feel?

Still, racism has helped me push myself to greater heights. Racism is just another form of pain, and without pain I'd never be where I am today. I use pain as an inspiration every single day. Some pains are intriguing and some pains are annoying. Some pains are sensitive. But I've realized the worst pain of all—the pain of not being free.

Until a few years ago, my life was a nightmare. I was of sound mind and body, but someone else was telling me what to do, how to do it and when to do it. It got to the point in my life that I had to stop. **I sat THERE and REFLECTED and REALIZED HOW FUCKED UP I WAS and THAT I HAD LOST A PART OF MY LIFE.**

When I see someone trapped in an existence like I was, it makes me sad. I want to help them. I want to tell them, **YOU HAVE THE KEYS TO YOUR FREEDOM, AND YOU MUST USE THEM.** Take someone like Princess Di. I feel for that woman. Watching her, I can tell she needs to have a wild guy that's very in control and sometimes out of control—someone who can make her life more exciting than it is. When you've got to be in front of the camera and be Mrs. Prissy all the time, it just eats away at your soul. Behind closed doors I'll bet she fucks like a raging bull. I'd love to find out. I think any man would love to take a shot at that challenge.

British society still hasn't broken away from some of the uptight bullshit that led the U.S. to claim independence in the first place. The Revolutionary War was one worth fighting, but most of the wars in my lifetime have been total bullshit. It's like that movie, *War Games*. That's all it is for the assholes who make the wars happen, but real people die, and that's harsh. I accept the fact that there will be clashes, but if they have to happen, here's how I think they should be settled: Take the ten toughest dudes in each country and put them in an enclosed space, like a miniature jungle, and let them go at it. The last country with at least one person standing wins the war. It would be great drama, and those people would be true national heroes And it would be a hell of a lot cheaper than maintaining an army and navy and air force and all that shit.

Would I go to war? Only if I had to. **If someone invaded this country I'd fight to protect my family. But would I have gone on Operation Desert Storm? No way.** I'd rather go to jail than put on a uniform and kill people just because I'm ordered to. And the way wars are these days, there's a good chance you'll get hit by chemical weapons or bombs or automatic gunfire or some other shit you have no chance in hell of surviving.

The two best things that came out of the sixties were the civil rights movement and the opposition to the Vietnam War. *I hope the kids today are as willing to rebel against something they think is wrong, and I'm pretty sure they are.* Kids today are taking their own authority. Kids are taking their own sense of direction. Kids aren't as straitlaced as they were in the eighties. They can do whatever they want to do, and they know it. That's another thing I love about America. It's a great nation that allows you to take off in search of adventure and return with no strings attached. You can **LOVE IT OR LEAVE IT**.

This country has a great history of people who walk away from their restrictive lives and just take off down the open road. I want to get a motorcycle and round up some crazy-ass people and take off across the country on a wild adventure. No plans, no publicity, just a random trip across this great nation of ours. I may even go this summer. Other people can follow us in a Winnebago or a car or whatever and we'll just party on down the road.

When it comes down to it, the ultimate freedom is to find the peace within yourself, and to live life to its fullest and discover its ultimate riches. DON'T GET CAUGHT UP IN ANY-THING. Just go from one page to the next and live day to day. You may be behind in someone else's count, but you'll definitely know that the mind's free of all the diversions and the aggravations and the bullshit. It's the simplest thing in the world to pull off, and yet it's also the hardest—even right here in the greatest country on earth.

Fifteen

Open Your Mind, Shock the System, and Rock the World

FEEL LIKE I'M A LIGHTNING ROD WHO CAN ABSORB ALL THE VENOM AND THE PAIN THIS WORLD HAS TO OFFER IN ORDER TO HELP PEOPLE WHO ARE MORE VULNERABLE. I get a lot of shit for a lot of what I do, but it doesn't bother me, because I can take it. I'm strong and successful and, finally, secure in my identity, so bring the shit on. ***Instead of bashing a gay guy you see on the street, come after me for being a drag-queen, boy-kissing fairy.*** And instead of ripping some poor black kid in the ghetto, beat on me for being an uppity N-word who loves to show his big black dong to white women.

Picture an electrical storm that's ripping through the air, and see me standing high above it all, sucking in all the energy and sending it back out to the people who need it most. It gives me a rush, because it tells me I can penetrate anything if I can take all that. And it jacks me up to know whose lives I might be impacting. `EVERY TIME I STAND UP FOR WHAT I BELIEVE IN, I HOPE THERE'S A SCARED, CONFUSED PERSON OUT THERE WHO WATCHES ME AND SMILES.` If I can show them that it's OK to go for it, that no amount of heat can bring you down if your convictions are strong, then maybe they'll be better able to strike back at the forces that are

240

keeping them down. We all have the power within us, but how many of us feel confident enough to use it? **LOOK AT ME: I WAS A SMALL MAN WHO STOLE CLOTHES AND FOOD AND NEEDED LOVE AND ATTENTION SO BADLY BUT WAS TOO SHY TO GET IT.**

Sometimes I'll be eating lunch or hanging out at a strip club or trying to sleep in the middle of the night and I'll see myself on TV, and I'll laugh out loud. **WHAT THE HELL AM I DOING HERE? I** SHOULD BE DEAD OR IN A DAL-LAS SLUM OR PLAYING CARDS WITH MY RED-NECK FRIENDS IN BOKCHITO. Was there a reason I became famous? Is it fate? Am I part of some master plan? I have no idea, but I do know my fame is something I absolutely cannot waste. It would be irresponsible, because a downtrod-den freak like me may never become famous again. *I HAVE TO GO OVER THE TOP AND LIVE WITH ABANDON.* There's a part of me that's goofing on the whole scene, and I want to milk it for all it's worth.

As long as I'm in position to live like a rock star, you're damn right **I'M GONNA ROCK THE WORLD.** Wouldn't you? It's a tough act to carry out at times, but as far as I'm con-cerned it's the only way to fly. A lot of celebrities don't air it out like I do because they're scared it will cost them their fame. I think that's bullshit, but even if I knew my fame was in jeopardy, so fucking what? If I fall from grace, will I be any lower than I was before? Hell, no. Besides, fame is always in jeopardy, as is life. *SECURITY IS AN ILLUSION.* People who think they can sustain something forever are just dreaming, and by worrying about it so much they fail to appreciate their good fortune while it's there.

Some people seem to think that I'm headed for a fall. Well, it's true: I may swan-dive right into a cesspool of fertilizer. If it happens tomorrow, it will be a rude awakening. It will be a bummer. But it will still be amazing—amazing that I had any-where to fall in the first place.

Think about it: If someone had told you a few years ago that I, a player who doesn't even score 10 points a game, would be one of the most famous athletes in the world, would you have believed it? What if that person also told you I would dye my hair pink and dress in women's clothes and kiss men and rock out onstage with Pearl Jam? You'd have thought that person was high as Timothy Leary. Hell, even if I fall, I still had a wild ride that nobody ever could have anticipated. I've still got a TV show and a movie and two books and a million stories. *I still fucked Madonna and a lot of other women who wouldn't have looked at me until a few years ago.* If I hit rock bottom, don't cry for me. Re-alize I've got a good thing going right know, and I'm appreciat-ing the hell out of it while it's happening. And, **IF I'M SUCCESSFUL IN MY MISSION, I'M USING MY FAME TO MAKE THIS WORLD A COOLER, LESS PAINFUL PLACE.**

There's a part of me that wants to help people who are less

fortunate by giving them money and attention. I give to chari-ties, and I hand out money to homeless people on the street practically every day. But realistically, how much of an impact am I making? There are so many charities in the world, and you can't give to every one. And you never know for sure where the money is going, if they're keeping it or not. That's why a lot of times I figure I might as well give my money directly to needy people. At least that's productive at the moment, and you know you've done something good. I've been there, so I know how good it feels when someone helps you out. A lot of people who give to the homeless want to make sure they're not using it to buy alcohol or drugs, but I could care less. Once I give them the money, what they do with it is their business. I'm trying to help them, not run their lives.

The homeless thing is so tough, and I know for damn sure I'm not gonna solve the problem. I always give them money, and the word is out. Now I feel like a bank at times. I'll be down on First Street in Chicago, and they'll be waiting for me to come out and then they'll hit me up. It's difficult to pass people up like that, but it's not like I'm a billionaire. Sometimes I have to say no. I'm not trying to be mean or rude, but I'll say, "I gave you twenty bucks yesterday. Please don't ask me again, OK?"

To make a positive impact, I have to think on a much bigger scale. **IF THERE'S ONE THING I CAN ACCOM-PLISH IN THIS LIFE, IT'S TO HELP IMPROVE THE REALITIES OF OTHERS BY BREAKING**

DOWN THE LAYERS OF SOCIETY'S BULLSHIT.

When I do that, it's like a great rush of freedom and fulfillment washes over me.

People who think I cross-dress or speak out for attention are missing the point. I don't need attention to get my point across. I do it for everybody else. I've gone through a long, hard struggle to get to this point, and now I don't need help like I used to. But other people do, so I'm trying to pave the way toward enlightenment and tolerance, because I'm in a position to do so.

Every day of my life, I try to inflict pain on myself mentally, physically, and emotionally. I see it as a challenge: Let me channel this pain within myself and then go out there and challenge everyone else. No one can hurt me then, because I've been through worse on my own. That's what the tattoos and the piercings are about—they're my way of testing myself to make sure I'm strong enough to handle everyone else's pain. I obviously have a very high tolerance for pain; if you've ever been tattooed, you know what I'm talking about. So I'll hold the pain, because I can, and because that's one of the main purposes for which I've been put on this earth.

It's not so much that I say things for shock value, it's that I'm very open to different ideas, and I think it's best to

Speak
Out
For
What
You
Believe
In.

It blows me away how scared most people are, especially famous people, to say something unpopular or controversial. All these people whose lives are so good and who have so much going for them feel like if they say something that's not totally vanilla, they'll somehow get stripped of all of it. They're completely paranoid, and I don't know why. ***IF YOU'RE WILLING TO SPEAK OUT AND STAND UP FOR WHAT YOU'VE SAID, IF YOU CARRY YOURSELF WITH PRIDE AND STRENGTH, WHO CARES IF YOUR STATEMENTS RUFFLE SOME FEATHERS?*** If your words strike a nerve, that's usually a sign that they're effective.

If there's one lesson I hope you take with you after reading this book, it's that the best thing you can do to improve this world is to **Wage War Against the Closed-Minded, Conservative, Control Freaks In Our Midst.** Free, imaginative thought is the essence of existence, and sometimes you have to put yourself out on a limb in order to break down the mental barriers in front of you. `Open Your Mind And Blow Other People's Minds In the Process.` If you believe that something is right, you shouldn't be ashamed to say or do it under any circumstances.

This country has an amazing history of people who changed society by being open-minded and bold. From the founding fathers to the civil-rights leaders of the sixties and beyond, people have been willing to stand up for views that were unpopular but which ultimately proved to be the correct way of thinking. Look at what people like Rosa Parks or Martin Luther King Jr. went through to get their point across. They didn't care if people yelled insults at them or threw stones or worse, it just made them stronger and more committed to the cause. **Martin Luther King Jr. and Malcolm X gave their lives because of other people's fear and small-mindedness.** But as the struggle continued and the hatred was exposed, people started seeing the big picture.

There are few things I hate more than people who can't see beyond their own little existence. I love it when someone rocks their worlds by doing something wild and sensational and impossible to ignore. I like people who get up in your face and make you think about issues. In the sixties, **JIMI HEN-DRIX, JIM MORRISON, AND JANIS JOPLIN WERE THREE OF THE COOLEST PERFORMERS** because they made people deal with their freakishness. Everything about them reeked of sex and drugs and loud-ass rock 'n roll and rebellion and passion. **THEY ALL GOT SO HARD-CORE INTO THEIR LIFESTYLES THAT THEY PAID WITH THEIR LIVES. IT'S ALMOST LIKE THEY HAD TO DIE YOUNG,** because of the era in which they were living. Back then, everyone was gonna push it as hard as they could until they flamed out; it was like a game of chicken with the whole world. But look how much Jimi, Janis, and Jim left us, and look at how much more accepted those things are in today's world because of them.

Another thing that the three of them did was, they had a hell of a good time. They fucked with people, and they made it fun. Jim Morrison got arrested for dropping his pants onstage. Jimi showed up on the Dick Cavett show barefoot and wearing a purple robe. CONSERVATIVE, UP-TIGHT PEOPLE TAKE THEMSELVES SO SERIOUSLY, and the best way to mess with them is to PUT IT BACK IN THEIR FACE WITH A COMIC TOUCH, and with a little satire thrown in.

I've done a lot of things to shock people in the past couple of years, and I have another surprise on the horizon. **SOME-TIME IN THE NEXT YEAR, I PLAN ON GOING DOWN TO THE COURTHOUSE AND LEGALLY CHANGING MY NAME FROM DENNIS K. RODMAN TO ORGASM.** Not Orgasm Rodman, or Dennis Orgasm, but Orgasm. I'll be the ultimate one-name wonder. **Eat your heart out Cleopatra, Fabian, Cher, Pele, Charo, Sting, and Madonna.**

Will I be doing this for attention? Of course. Will I be doing it for comic value, another antic in the name of public theater? **ABSOLUTELY.** But there will be another, more important purpose. Changing my name to Orgasm, and forcing people to deal with the most awesome feeling in the world, will help me prove a point about the uptight nature of our society. **It will provoke debate about the taboo of SEXUAL OPENNESS.** It will do for the word "orgasm" what the Bob-

"OUR NEXT GUEST IS . . . ORGASM."

bitt incident did for the word "penis." It will boost TV ratings and leave a lasting tattoo on the NBA.

Life's too short not to have fun. My friends may not be the most noble people in the world, but one thing they all have in common is they attack life and refuse to let themselves get bogged down by pettiness and bullshit. When we get together, there's a rush of energy in the air that screams out, "Here we come, we're taking over this town right now, so come along or get the hell out of the way." **THERE'S AN URGENCY TO OUR BEHAVIOR BECAUSE WE KNOW LIFE IS PRECIOUS AND FLEETING AND IT'S JUST TOO DAMN DEPRESSING TO STAND ON THE SIDELINES.**
We jump right into the middle of the action and are always open to adventure, and conservative people hate us for that. They hate us because they're scared. So many people are raised to be close-minded, and they shut themelves off to possibilities. They're afraid to open up to what makes them excited and what makes them happy. **Everyone has that wild streak in their body.** Everyone is like, "I want to be FREE. I want to be stress free, problem free, and free of restrictions." But they're afraid to step out and walk on the wild side.
I'm not just talking about letting loose and having fun. *PEO-PLE SHOULD OPEN THEIR MINDS TO WHAT'S HAPPENING IN THIS WORLD, FROM RACISM TO POLITICS TO ALL ASPECTS OF*

LIFE IN GENERAL. People have this notion that life should be a certain way. They don't understand that they're sitting behind a two-way mirror, watching what their life could be if they just followed their freaky instincts.

I'm open to so many different concepts that my mind is like a whirlwind with thoughts rushing through it all the time. My basic philosophy is, DON'T RULE ANYTHING OUT. I laugh when people say there's no life beyond earth. Yeah, right. Think of how small the earth is within the galaxy, not to mention the universe. It's arrogant to think that it's just us, that there's nothing else out there.

I believe in UFOs. I believe the military has aliens and spaceships stashed away because they don't want to freak people out. But it wouldn't freak me out. I think there's some crazy shit out in the stratosphere. Hell, I think there's some crazies on this earth that we don't know about.

You start wondering why certain things happen and why things disappear from your eyes or appear out of nowhere. There have to be some extraterrestrial forces at work. To me it's not scary, it's interesting as hell. If I could meet an alien, I know that after a while I'd be able to make the motherfucker understand what the hell I was saying.

You bet your ass I believe in ghosts. That's one reason I won't fuck in a cemetery. I've felt ghosts pass through my spirit before. It's just an expression of energy through your body. It can be right behind you, doing everything you're doing, and you can feel it, but you can't touch it—the ghost has a hold of you.

To me `EVERYTHING IS POSSIBLE.` I spend so much time analyzing and visualizing, thinking of things that have happened in the past and things that are gonna happen in the future. It's like **MY HEAD IS ALWAYS ON FIRE.** Of all people, Madonna may have summed up my mental process best. She was trying to insult me, because she was pissed off about the stuff I revealed about our sexual encounters, and she said I was crazy. Here's her actual quote, from an interview with *Vogue* magazine: "He is someone I would classify as a border-line psychotic personality. He is a very exciting person to be around, like most crazy people, and during the whole two months I dated him . . . it was like this fun adventure, and then I soon discovered that he was a seriously damaged person, and I really couldn't get away from him fast enough. Much as I should hate him, I actually feel compassion for him. This is a person with a few screws loose."

My defense? Nothing to say, bro. **It doesn't hurt my feelings that she said that.** A lot of people say she has some screws loose, with all the crazy shit she's been into. But to me, **being called crazy is a compliment.** I'd rather be considered crazy than mentally dull, and she's right: it does make things a lot more exciting.

Am I really crazy, in a clinical sense? I don't think so. **I'VE BEEN TO SEE PSYCHOLOGISTS BEFORE.** They've all told me I'm not crazy. They said I was very well-rounded and that I have my shit together. But even if they said

I was totally insane, I wouldn't put much stock in it. People that get paid to pick your mind have nothing better to do in their lives. I don't need to figure out the mind; **I DON'T WANT TO BE GOD.** Only one person knows what's going on in my mind, and we know who that is.

Instead of wasting our time and energy trying to slap a definition on shit we can't understand, let's go out and live and worry about the ramifications and classifications later. History will be written and retold and preserved through pictures and videotapes and memories, no matter how hard we try to catch it as it happens. But we can't catch it; all we can do is be it. Eventually, time is going to kick all of our asses. **The only way to cope is to do as much as you can with as much zest as you can and smile and yell and scream and cry and love your way through it.**

It sounds difficult and complicated, but it doesn't have to be a struggle at all. **EVERYTHING YOU NEED TO SET YOURSELF FREE IS RIGHT THERE INSIDE OF YOU.** If you close your eyes and concentrate, you can feel it in the blood rushing through your veins and the thumping of your heart. WHEN YOU CAN FEEL YOUR INNER SPIRIT THEN PEACE WILL OVERCOME YOU, AND YOU'LL BE READY TO BREAK THROUGH THAT MIRROR OR FLY THROUGH THAT WINDOW AND FLOURISH. Or it may be something as simple as opening up a door and stepping into a land you've been check-ing out all along. **THE WILD SIDE MAY BE RIGHT THERE IN FRONT OF YOU.**

WALK ON THE WILD SIDE.

ACKNOWLEDGMENTS

To Leslie, my wild child, for making it all possible.

This book was facilitated by the strength of my family: Leslie, Natalie, and Dr. J. Silver, who give me love in its rawest form; Stephen and Susan Silver, to whom I owe everything; Elizabeth Silver, who keeps my brain warm; the amazing Goyettes; Mark Tourgeman and family; and Sonny and Laura Feldman. Thanks to: Mike Fleiss, for the constant inspiration; Bill Colson and the Powers That Be at *SI*, for the opportunity; Mark Godich, Peter King, and Austin Murphy, for carrying me; Janet Pawson—we did this, finally; Leslie Schnur and Jacob Hoye, for making it sing; Val Highsmith, interpreter; Rick Telander, Gonzo God; Dwight Manley, for your trust.

And Worm—thanks for having the balls to walk on the wild side, and for being a true friend.

—M.S.

PHOTO CREDITS

BILL SMITH: PP. 4, 8, 10, 13, 19, 24, 25, 31, 38, 41, 43, 47, 49, 57, 61, 73, 79, 92, 113, 118, 125, 130, 137, 141, 147, 154, 156, 169, 175, 178, 181, 184, 209, 217, 220, 223, 249, 254, 255, 256

ALBERT WATSON: PP. 1, 17, 35, 45, 59, 71, 75, 82, 83, 86, 91, 109, 121, 145, 161, 173, 189, 221, 225, 239

DWIGHT MANLEY: PP. 34, 122, 208, 257, 258

JOHN MCDONOUGH: P. 231